THE SHIP FOR KOBE

A memoir

GUERNICA WORLD EDITIONS 98

CENTRO
PER IL LIBRO
E LA LETTURA

We acknowledge and are grateful for the support of
IL CENTRO PER IL LIBRO E LA LETTURA

THE SHIP FOR KOBE

A memoir

DACIA MARAINI

Translated by GENNI GUNN

GUERNICA
World
EDITIONS
TORONTO—CHICAGO—BUFFALO—LANCASTER (U.K.)
2025

Guernica Editions Founder: Antonio D'Alfonso

Michael Mirolla, editor
Cover design: Allen Jomoc Jr.
Interior design: Jill Ronsley, suneditwrite.com

Guernica Editions Inc.
1241 Marble Rock Rd., Gananoque (ON), Canada K7G 2V4
2250 Military Road, Tonawanda, N.Y. 14150-6000 U.S.A.
www.guernicaeditions.com

Distributors:
Independent Publishers Group (IPG)
600 North Pulaski Road, Chicago IL 60624
University of Toronto Press Distribution (UTP)
5201 Dufferin Street, Toronto (ON), Canada M3H 5T8

First edition.
Printed in Canada.

Legal Deposit—First Quarter
Library of Congress Catalog Card Number: 2024944591
Library and Archives Canada Cataloguing in Publication
Title: The ship for Kobe : a memoir / Dacia Maraini.
Other titles: Nave per Kobe. English
Names: Maraini, Dacia, author.
Series: Guernica world editions (Series) ; 98.
Description: First edition. | Series statement: Guernica world editions ; 98 |
Translation of: La nave per Kobe: diari giapponesi di mia madre.
Identifiers: Canadiana (print) 20240446712 | Canadiana (ebook)
20240446747 | ISBN 9781778490019 (softcover) | ISBN 9781778490026 (EPUB)
Subjects: LCSH: Maraini, Dacia—Family. | LCSH: Alliata, Topazia,
1913-2015—Diaries. | LCSH:
Authors, Italian—20th century—Family relationships. | LCSH: Authors,
Italian—20th century—Travel— Japan. | LCSH: Authors, Italian—20th
century—Biography. | LCGFT: Autobiographies.
Classification: LCC PQ4873.A69 Z46513 2025 | DDC 853/.914—dc23

My ship laden with oblivion
sails on a bitter sea, at midnight in winter
[…] The sail torn by a gust of humid eternal
sighs, of hope and desire.
　　　　—**Francesco Petrarca,** *Le rime*

Memories, those exceedingly long shadows
of our brief body.
　　　　—**Vincenzo Cardarelli,** "Passato," *Poesie*

WATER is taught by thirst;
Land, by the oceans passed;
Transport, by throe;
Peace, by its battles told;
Love, by memorial moul;
Birds, by the snow.
　　　　—**Emily Dickinson,** *Complete Poems*

Introduction

Memory and Travelling in Maraini's
La nave per Kobe.

Michelangelo La Luna
University of Rhode Island

I. Japan 1938-1945

1. The first three years in Japan (1938-1941).

On October 18, 1938, Fosco Maraini, Topazia Alliata and their two-years old baby Dacia embarked on the Conte Verde to go from Brindisi to Shanghai, and then on the Corfù, a less comfortable English boat, that took them to Kobe, Japan. After a few days in Tokyo, they went to Sapporo where, thanks to a Kokusai Gakuyu Kai scholarship, Fosco was to conduct research at the University of Hokkaido with Professor S. Kodama, on the Ainu indigenous population (also known as the "white people" of Japan).

The first few years spent in the Northern part of the Hokkaido island were very happy for the Marainis. Meanwhile the family grew larger with Yuki born in Sapporo in 1939, and Antonietta, called Toni, born in Tokyo, in 1941. Dacia grew up speaking English with Topazia, who in turn had learned it from her British nannies, like many members of the noble Sicilian families. Moreover, Daciuzza (this was a term of endearment used by her mother) spoke Japanese with her playmates and her nanny Sawako Morioka, who played a very important role in her childhood, as she states in a 1990 article regarding her return to Nagoya:

1

"The first person we meet in Nagoya is Sawako Morioka, the nurse who held me and my sisters in her arms during the war years. She is small, eighty years old, but her cheeks are still rosy and her laugh cheerful. We hug. We exchange gifts. Unfortunately, I no longer speak Japanese and her Italian is incomprehensible. 'Stanco biaggio?' ('Tired trip?') she repeats, massaging my aching neck. Her fingers run quick and wise. I think back to how she was when she was young, robust, small, festive, able to go carry my sister Toni tied to her back, my sister Yuki in her arms, and me pulled by the hand. She was the only one who dared to challenge the police so she could visit us in the concentration camp. And for this, she was beaten and warned."[1]

2. *The beginning of the war and the end of Topazia's diaries (1941-1943).*

The situation began to change with the attack of the US fleet at Pearl Harbor in the Hawaiian Islands, on December 7, 1941, which marked Japan's entry into the war. In 1942, Fosco obtained a position of lecturer of Italian at the University of Kyoto, therefore he and his family moved to the "Thousand-Year Capital." At that time, the Japanese authorities began to keep the Italians under control, and Topazia stopped writing her diary, probably for fear of being accused of espionage. Everything changed radically with Badoglio's proclamation of the Armistice. In fact, on September 9, 1943, the Japanese police swooped into Marainis' house to ask if they were on the side of the King of Italy or of Mussolini, and received the following reply:

"What would you Japanese do in such a case? - we asked the officer - Would you stay with the Emperor or the Prime Minister? " "Obviously with the emperor!" was the immediate reply. «Well we too imitate you, we are with the King» «In which case we are very sorry - the inspector said rising - mais vous devenez ennemis... and you will have to suffer the consequences. Prepare for internment».[2]

At first, Maraini's parents were placed under house arrest, but after refusing to join the Republic of Salò (founded by Mussolini on September 23, 1943), they were considered traitors and enemies. During that period, Fosco had to find a way to save his books, pictures and other ethnographic material he had collected during the five years he spent in Japan:

"I had already collected a thousand volumes, as well as a lot of ethnographic material. I closed it all in about fifty fireboxes (as they used to do in Japan at the time) hoping that some miracle would save them. And the miracle happened! Meanwhile, the vice-director of the French Cultural Institute in Kyoto, our friend Jean-Pierre Hauchecorne (unfortunately recently deceased) came to our aid and took away the boxes and hid them in the large cellars of the institute itself."[3]

In one of the fifty boxes used to store ethnographic material were the two notebooks written by Topazia: a brown one entitled "DACIA: Dal 31 ott. 1938 al 30 giugno 1939," ("DACIA: From October 31, 1938, to June 30, 1939,"), and a red one entitled "Topazia, Dacia, Yuki, Toni – 1939-1941." These diaries about her daughters Topazia kept for the first three years in Japan, and included notes of their daily life, pictures, and maps. Here it is how Dacia Maraini explains when and why her mother stopped writing her diaries:

"1942. My mother's diary is now silent. She can't recall if she kept any trace of the daily news of 1942 and 1943, before entering the camp, where there certainly would have been no way to write or read. 'Perhaps I stopped keeping the diary about my daughters because the climate had changed. We lived in apprehension. The newspapers repeated words ordered by the government. And the people said, 'Hitar, psuyoi-né,' Hitler is powerful, right? with a mixture of admiration and fear.'"[4]

3. The Tempaku camp and the person-books (1943- 1945).

Toward the end of October 1943, the Marainis were transferred, together with other Italian anti-fascists, to the internment camp of Tempaku, located in one of the sixteen districts of Nagoya. At first, the local authorities wanted to place the three daughters in an institution, but thanks to the intervention of the wife of the mayor of the capital, who was a Christian and a friend of the family, they were left to their parents.

In the internment camp there were no books and therefore Topazia and Fosco played the role of "person-books" – as Maraini herself likes to call them, recalling the novel *Fahrenheit 451* – who told their little girls many fairy tales:

"Do you know the famous novel *Fahrenheit 451*, published by Ray Bradbury in 1953? It presents a dictatorship, which abolishes all books and burns them, like the Nazi's used to do. So, what did the people in that situation do? They started to learn the classics by heart. There were no books, but there were people, person-books. I found this to be an extraordinary idea ... So the first two books of my life were my father and my mother ... In the concentration camp my mother recounted the *Pinocchio* tale many times and she also talked about Grimm's *Fairy Tales* and about *Cappuccetto Rosso (Little Red Riding Hood)*, etc."[5]

The years of imprisonment in Tempaku were very hard: in addition to the fear of being slaughtered by the Japanese, or of dying under the the Allies' bombing, the Marainis suffered starvation, were attacked by parasites and worms of all kinds, and were subject to continuous diseases, including beriberi, scurvy, dysentery, mumps, etc. Perhaps some of them would have died without Fosco's *yubikiri*: on July 17, 1944, he cut off his little finger and threw it as a sign of defiance to the cruelest of guards, who then reacted violently. After a few days, however, the guard brought him a goat as a sign of admiration for the deed, which was inspired by an ancient samurai tradition. It was thanks to the milk produced by the goat that the girls were able to survive the harshest period of confinement (July 1944-May 1945).[6]

4. Kosaiji, Tokyo and Florence (1945-1946).

On May 8, 1945, the prisoners had to leave the Tempaku camp to move to Kosaiji, next to the Buddhist temple of Nagoya. Two weeks after the end of the War and the surrender of the Japanese Empire (August 15, 1945), Dacia and her family were rescued by the American troops and transferred from Kosaiji to Tokyo, where Fosco worked as an interpreter for the American VIII Army, and Topazia as an expert in works of art for the AECPO – Army Exchange Central Purchasing Office. In the Spring of 1946, the US Navy offered them a free trip to return to Europe. With them, they brought the 50 boxes hidden at the French Cultural Institute. Everything was incredibly intact, because the Allies did not destroy Kyoto, the most important cultural and religious center of Japan, also known as the "city of a thousand temples":

> "It was a very long crossing of two oceans; first the Pacific, then the Panama Canal, finally the Atlantic with the last landing in the French port of Le Havre. The journey from Le Havre to Florence still remained ... Here another lucky event: the Italian ambassador, with whom we were travelling, added our luggage and the famous 50 boxes to the mission cargo. In short, by May 1946, from miracle to miracle we were in Florence without having lost anything - and with the sole expense of a few tips to the various porters

along the way. The ethnographic collection was donated by me shortly afterwards to the Anthropology Museum at Palazzo Nonfinito; and the core of the library was safe in the family home, outside Porta Romana, in Florence."[7]

II.   Memory and *La nave per Kobe*.

1. *The narrative and importance of the book.*

We can consider *La nave per Kobe* as one of the most important books written by Dacia Maraini, because it constitutes a sort of a bridge through which the author makes her first steps back toward that period of WWII (1943-1945), with which she would like to complete her sixty-year long career as a writer:

> "Before I die, I want to write a book about my experience in the concentration camp. I've written something, but not everything about all the occurrences in the camp; the experience of hunger, fear, etc., but until now I couldn't really write about it. So, you see the distance of time that you need in front of the distance of the narration, which are two kinds of distances, but maybe a writer deals with them both."[8]

The eight years spent in Japan constituted for the Marainis an indelible memory that they tried to recall through their writings, especially Fosco who wrote most of his books on Japan, among which of mention are *Ore giapponesi*, 1957, and *Case, amori, universi*, 1999.

When Dacia received Topazia's travelogues[9] from Fosco (in about 2000), she didn't really know what to do with them, primarily because for years she had tried to remove from her memory the pain and deprivation she had gone through as a child during the last period she spent in Japan. In the beginning of *La nave per Kobe*, Dacia Maraini admits that she thought those years for her were dead forever, but thanks to the text and pictures in her mother's diaries, she realizes that they were just asleep in a corner of her memory. Moreover, the writer states that she doesn't recognize Daciuzza and what she did, almost as if she has nothing to do with her anymore:

"The past has the capacity to ambush you through a photograph, a letter. It recounts a time that no longer exists, yet materializes in front of you, surprisingly vivid and full-bodied. It conjures in your ear a part of you that vanished long ago, that you thought dead, and instead was hibernating in a corner of your memory. I am this child, I tell myself, but she is no longer me."[10]

This creates a sort of narratological split that allows Maraini to proceed backwards and forwards, springing from an episode described in Topazia's diaries to an episode of her life, and vice versa. Moreover, the notebooks often lead Dacia into insightful commentary and reflection. This dialectic way of progressing helps Dacia to slowly repossess the memory of a dormant past, and ultimately to regain her confidence with that part of herself that will eventually allow her to complete her literary journey.

The difficulties of sailing in the ocean of her memories are also evident from some of the epigraphs that Maraini places in the beginning of the book, quoting lines by poets such as Petrarca and Caldarelli who emphasize how complicated it is to resume painful reminiscences of our past:

"My ship laden with oblivion
sails on a bitter sea, at midnight in winter
[…] The sail torn by a gust of humid eternal
sighs, of hope and desire."[11]

[1] *"Memories, those exceedingly long shadows of our brief body"*[12]

7

It is the same suffering mixed with fear that the writer admits experiencing each time she tries to approach "the edge of the woods," by trying to remember the years she spent in Japan, as she states at the end of the book:

> "Therefore, I ask my readers to be patient to listen to what follows the events thus far: the years in the concentration camp, so intense and painful, the war, the daily life of the camp. For many years, I tried to tell this story, but I have always paused, breathless, at the edge of the woods, in both shame and dismay. Suddenly In front of me appears a face-less man, who walks quickly. And I run, run, until I reach a truck and I tell the driver about the terrible encounter. And he turns his empty face towards me, and says, "'Like me?'"[13]

III. Travelling and La nave per Kobe.

1. *Io sono nata viaggiando.*

Io sono nata viaggiando (*I Was Born Travelling*) is the title of the 2013 documentary written and directed by Irish Braschi on Dacia Maraini's life, which speaks not only about the countries she visited, but also about the concepts of travelling-time-memory, and how they are connected with writing and literature. As it happens in similar autobiographical books such as *Bagheria, La grande festa, La seduzione dell'altrove*, in *La nave per Kobe* travelling constitutes the best way through which Maraini connects her childhood in Japan/her mom's diaries with herself.

The Conte Verde and the Corfù's stopover ports indicated in the map drawn by Topazia, as well as the people that she mentioned in her diaries, offer Dacia the opportunity to discuss her own trips: it doesn't matter whether they were real trips, or ones imagined through movies, photographs, novels etc. The first stop the Conte Verde made was Porto Said, a place that Dacia's parents didn't like to visit because they were afraid to contract an infection. Although Dacia never visited that place, she speaks about it looking at some pictures of the Hotel Victoria in which there are "women in long skirts, umbrellas in hand, as if they have just stepped out of a Chekov story." Then she completes her imaginary trip by connecting the hotel hall with a similar hall in the movie *Casablanca*, where she would meet an Ingrid Bergman, whose beauty and features remind her of Topazia:

> "Later, in a room like that one, I would come to know through film, the Ingrid Bergman of suffused light reflected in soft eyes, of chestnut curls flickering around her neck. What enchantment binds us to an actress with a delicate smile and a crystal-clear voice? In her, I saw my young mother: the slender legs, the cut of her suit cinched at the waist, the wedge-heeled shoes. I saw her walking quickly, in a brown felt hat that partly covered her forehead, and I felt as if I were watching an entire generation of women with secret steps and sparkling eyes."[14]

2. Travelling with Alberto Moravia and Pier Paolo Pasolini.

In *La nave per Kobe* striking are the trips that Dacia took with Alberto Moravia and Pier Paolo Pasolini, for whom travelling was an essential part of their being, just as literature was: it was also a way to enlarge their knowledge and ideas, to collect material and inspiration for writing. Moravia gives us a very good idea of how great it was travelling with Dacia Maraini, in comparison with his previous partner, the writer Elsa Morante:

> "Elsa gave her best in exceptional, emergency circumstances. But in her travels she had the particularity of bringing with her the psychological relationship that is typical of everyday life. We could also go to the end of the world, but it seemed that we were still in Via dell'Oca. She

did not travel, Elsa, she moved, that's all. With Dacia, on the other hand, I truly traveled, in a somewhat adventurous sense that is not so much made up of adventures, but of complete forgetfulness of the stable and well-defined world left at home... I traveled as we dream ... I finally traveled with abandonment and discovery. It is not without significance that to celebrate our union we chose to go around the world. Maybe it was some kind of gamble; in reality it was also above all a finally satisfied hunger for space and freedom."[15]

A missionary, padre Rovelli, who Topazia describes as being very nice and friendly with her daughter, brings back to memory an incident in Africa that happened during a trip in which the Land Rover of the three writers broke in the middle of nowhere. Fortunately a Mercedes passed by, carrying a bishop, who invited them to get in and to stay at his mission only 20 kilometers away. At dinner they were surprised to realize that the bishop did not know who Moravia and Pasolini were, but that he knew all the names of the players of the Roma soccer team. The most disappointing aspect of this experience is that the day after, when they were ready to leave and to give a gratuity to the mission, they were asked to pay for room and board, as if they had stayed in a four-star hotel:

> "But just at that moment, the bishop's clerk arrives, dressed in black on black—very elegant—and hands us a bill. We are flabbergasted. The bishop has accounted for even the water we used for washing, and the total comes to about the price of a four-star hotel! What small offering! We pay and leave, without even seeing him, the bishop who, at ten o'clock in the morning, is still asleep."[16]

What exemplifies the importance and essence of travel for Maraini, Moravia and Pasolini, is the fact that each time they made a trip, they would read literature or travelogues to get a better sense of the places they were visiting. After commenting on Topazia's diary, which said that she and Fosco had visited Bombay while Dacia was left asleep in the care of a waiter, Maraini informs us that when she visited the city in 1964, she read *A passage to India* by Forester during the hot days in which they could go out of the hotel only at 5am, or after 9pm. Moravia and Pasolini had already been in India twice and they had written several articles about it, later collected respectively in the 1962 books *Un'idea dell'India* (*An idea of India*) and *L'odore dell'India* (*The smell of India*): the first spoke more objectively and rationally about India and how religion is able to unify the country, the latter was deeply touched by the misery of the place and gave a more passionate, intimate, instinctive description of it.[17]

Among other things, in *La nave per Kobe* Dacia remembers the madras cotton shirts that they got in Bombay (you could order and have them done in two hours) that they wore for several years and that she still keeps at home.[18]

IV.   Genni Gunn translation of *La nave per Kobe*

3. A conversation with Genni Gunn.

For this Introduction I asked Genni Gunn some questions to help the reader better understand why and how she translated *La nave per Kobe*.

Michelangelo La Luna: Can you please explain why you like to translate Italian authors, and what kind of experience you have with it?

Genni Gunn: Italian is my mother tongue, yet English is the language in which I write. Translation has always been a way to keep me connected to my mother tongue, and to use my poetic (I've translated two of Dacia's poetry collections and one of Corrado Calabró's) and literary skills in English to render literary works from Italian. I read somewhere that we store our mother tongue in a different part of the brain from any languages we learn after the age of about seven or eight. People like me, who came to Canada early enough may have stored both languages in the mother tongue part of the brain.

MLL: What is your approach to language?

GG: Just as there are no two words in the English language which have the exact same meaning, no word has its exact equivalent in another language. Words carry with them the atmosphere and rhythm of a cultural, historical and aesthetic tradition. It's not enough to translate words or phrases as one would find them in the dictionary. The translator has to recognize that each word represents a concept, that it reflects an emotional landscape. My work then, is to interpret that concept in relation to the sentence, and to the rest of the work in general, before making a decision about how to render the original into the target language.

MLL: What kind of approach did you use, did you do a literary translation, or a more creative one?

GG: I did a literary translation, trying to preserve the author's style without making the translation sound stilted and awkward. I tried to pay attention to the rhythm of the original.

Once I had a coherent literal, I began to concentrate on the structural differences between English and Italian, the significance of tone and style, the author's voice. Some of this I may already have done during the process of creating the literal; some I had to shape and change now. For example, if the author used a clipped style, with short sentences and simple words, I would try to re-create that in the English. If the author used long sentences and a rich vocabulary, I would try to be faithful to that. Naturally, much of this structural work is to some degree a creative effort, and would differ from translator to translator.

MLL: How did you translate the Italian and Japanese words?

GG: Some of the baby words, I left as they were, because it was easy to decipher what they were saying:

Yuki tried to sing! Hilarious. I've never heard a 10-month old baby try to do anything but talk. Now she says, "ittai" and "ba" and "Uchi-chan" as well as "tata, dada, bab, ciacia."19

In other instances, I also left the Japanese, because in the Italian the Japanese would also be foreign. I just made sure that the context gave us the meaning. Such as:

D. is very interested in meeting so many Italian children – but she hardly speaks! After 40 days in Tokyo, she has already learned a lot of Italian! Everyone finds her so good, so polite. "What a treasure of a child!" With the Japanese children, she is much more naughty, perhaps because she feels at home with them – and they laugh and say "kawaii" no matter what she does! In the hotel, D. befriended everyone. She received gifts from everyone, soldiers, (officers), ladies, waitresses, lift boys! I am extremely mortified!20

"Kawaii" means "cute" and the meaning here is easily understood, even if not exact. In some instances, I made a footnote if that was necessary.

MLL: What kind of difficulties did you find?

GG: The most difficult was the nonsense poem the father made up. So I left the nonsense words and adjusted them and made up new ones so that I could preserve the rhyme in English:

"Oh aunts oh sweet aunts in *bardocheta*
turn within the embroidered *glime*
descend the stairs *beta beta*
from the *maberi* of fused time!

Who knows if down there *the sobite*
Slowly *gramugna* in *cantalaghi*
in the *ufe coccia ccoccia* of the night?
Now it's no use going out on the *sbaghi*
staring ahead with haughty air,
among the *lugheri,* the *archostoñ,* the *snaghi.*"[21]

MLL: How long did you take to complete the job?

GG: I completed the work in about 6 months. First I read the work in Italian, and noted any words or concepts I wasn't sure of. Then I did a literal translation, including context in brackets as much as possible for anything that was vague. Then I began the first draft, keeping both literal and original visible. I spent a lot of time in dictionaries and thesauruses, sometimes for hours, trying to find the exact right word or phrase.

MLL: Why did you do it?

GG: Ever since I first was introduced to Dacia's work in the mid-1980s, and got to know her as a friend, I have felt a deep affinity with her sensibility. Interesting enough, the more I read her works, and as I translated her memoir, I was startled to discover our many similarities. We are both travelers, and were displaced as children. And our worldview is very similar.

MLL: What do you expect from it?

GG: I would like Dacia's work to be much more known to English speakers. Although she is well-known in Europe, I don't think she's as well known here. I know she is known in NY and California, certainly in universities that have Italian departments. She was discussing women's issues that are prominent today, as far back as the 1960s. I think her work is totally relevant in this moment. For example, there has been a spate of books published recently such as

Olga Tokarczuk's *Drive Your Plow Over the Bones of the Dead*, and Karen Joy Fowler's *we are all completely beside ourselves*, that discuss the plight of animals and our dysfunctional relationship to them. Dacia is a vegetarian and has been discussing this for many years:

> "Nature, or God, created carnivorous men, created hunters, many say, in the sublime presumption that the human race is superior to any other living being on earth. But, but… the doubts are many and are born the moment that science discovers, almost against its own will, a complex and varied animal world, in which intelligence and the capacity to communicate are daily discovered to be bolder and more imaginative."[22]

In the 1960s, Dacia Maraini was at the forefront of feminism and activism. She visited women's prisons, wrote articles and novels and plays and established an all-women theatre company. Her concerns were and continue to be much the same as those that concern our society today: gender inequality, abortion, spousal abuse, gender violence, maternity." Our @MeToo moment is fresh, yet Dacia has always been concerned with the lives of women, the lack of freedom, of equality, with the betrayal of men:

> "It's this, you know, that historically has aggravated the condition of women," my historian friend tells me. A girl who has aged prematurely by making waves, and is called in a derogatory tone 'the feminist.' "They're considered important for reproduction, but to be kept under control, demonized when they show autonomy in pleasure, made complicit in their submission, with detailed teaching that instills in their hearts the idea of belonging to a lower, weaker, more unreliable, more dangerous, more restless, more sentimental race, and therefore in need of guidance, protection, precise directives. Here she is, Woman, dear Dacia, who gets angry, who denigrates herself, who throws

herself away, who distresses herself, who feels guilty ... do you feel sorry for her? I can't hate her, however, you know, never, not even when she gets angry and sows traps for the unfortunate. The 'gold diggers,' for example, as the Americans call them, the young ladies of fortune, the femme fatales. Not even those can I condemn. It's the low self-esteem, the long practice of enmity towards other women that has made them like this, whether they're good or bad, they don't know it. They are absolutely blind and they have a great desire to live. They believe they are maneaters, and don't realize that they will always be eaten, because the male they think they dominate, considers them a little sordid, a little wicked, a little treacherous, a little deadbeat, a little dangerous, a little different, but all together so much, so much so, as to want to eliminate them."[23]

The Ship for Kobe is an introduction to Maraini's voice, to her past and to her peripatetic life. She is truly, as the *Guardian* noted, "a novelist of grand ambition and intense feeling and, always, an enthralling storyteller."

Notes

Except for the quotations from *La nave per Kobe* (translations by Genni Gunn) and unless otherwise specified, all translations in this Introduction from Italian into English are by Michelangelo La Luna.

The Italian quotations from *La nave per Kobe* come from the edition BUR Contemporanea, Rizzoli, 2012.

One day, my father handed me these notebooks, saying, "These are about you. Take them." I began to leaf through them, and as I proceeded, I was overwhelmed by emotion. The past has the capacity to ambush you through a photograph, a letter. It recounts a time that no longer exists, yet materializes in front of you, surprisingly vivid and full-bodied. It conjures in your ear a part of you that vanished long ago, that you thought dead, and instead was hibernating in a corner of your memory. I am this child, I tell myself, but she is no longer me. I've lost forever the body that appears so real in that photograph, so crisp and consistent. Today, this new body—worn, injured by time and experience, wounded like an old soldier who has seen too many wars—sits in the sun, trying to warm the blood that circulates with maddening lethargy.

What has this distant child to do with me?

I admit I don't much care for her. She's dead. Too bad. It took such effort to outgrow her, that I almost consider her a distant enemy.

What caused me pain back then, and fosters it today, is the loss of my mother's youth, so fresh and tender and distant. My mother's youth is almost more dear to me than mine and an integral part of the spiritual mythology I claim in order to believe in reality.

As a child, someone, perhaps my nanny Masako Moriokan, called Okachan, explained that I had to sleep, because while sleeping I would grow. But then, without a touch of malice, she added that my growing would make my mother age, and this was a natural progression: my child feet would lengthen, strengthen, and with small gentle strokes, would push my mother closer to old age.

This both alarmed and hurt me. The idea that my mother would age because of me was intolerable, and I searched for strategies to stop the time which pushed me towards adolescence and my mother towards old age. Therefore, I was inhabited by an insistent nagging: how could I not grow, or at least slow down this cruel and thoughtless growth?

The solution, I thought I understood, was to not sleep. If sleeping meant that I would grow, and my growth meant the shortening of my mother's youth, the only possible solution was to give up sleep. That way, I could remain a child and my mother would remain on the threshold of youth: a joyful, gentle woman, sure-footed, with hands always in motion. So smiling and cheerful. So necessary for the balance of my thoughts and so indispensable to the fullness of my trust in the world and in the family.

I believe that's where my insomnia originated, something I've always suffered, and which at times, persists with radical tenacity. I tend to sleep little, and when I do sleep, a breath can awaken me, as if each hour lost in sleep is still today an offense against the fullness and gaiety of my mother.

What sorrow to know that my strategies served nothing. Even if my mother looks ten years younger than her age, even if she has a steady voice, thick hair, once brown, that began to grey in her 80s, and is still not all white. Even if her judgment is lucid and firm. It's no wonder that when I have too much to do, I consign new books to her, so that she can read them and shortlist the best for me. Her comments are intelligent and current. She has no prejudices, my mother. The young woman growing old is still at the forefront of issues affecting our civil society. And yet, I have not been able to stop her from becoming smaller and more fragile, from acquiring wrinkles and pains like any elderly person.

October 31, 1938. We are embarking at Brindisi on the "Conte Verde," writes my mother in her diary: *Grandma Yoi gave Dacia a little, almost–boyish grey coat that looks adorable.*

You can still hear the Palermo cadences in my mother's words. The young Sicilian whose parents would have wanted her to marry a count flees with a Florentine boy with no prospects or assets, blond, strong, a cowlick skimming his forehead—who is in love with my mother, quarrelling with his father.

Departure is sad, and we're all extremely tired. Dacia has not slept enough and is difficult and irritable.

My wonderful father, Fosco, just graduated from university, penniless, rich only of a modest but exciting scholarship, stood on the ship's bridge and watched the foaming sea as if he expected to see a dragon fish with giant ears. The young Topazia tenderly leaned her chin on his shoulder, as if to help him chase away the nostalgia for Italy, for Florence, for his beloved mother, for the house in Torre di Sopra. Who knows if he was recalling how he had fought with his father who had offered him a job and a Fascist card, how he had ripped it into a thousand pieces right there, before his father's eyes.

We are not seasick, my mother writes and she was certainly sincere, but I find this equally curious, because I've always suffered from seasickness. Is it possible that when one is a little more than a year old, one does not experience nausea? Or was it due to the fact that only the surface of the sea was battered by the wind, and the large iron belly sailed on those waves with quiet determination, without excessive jolts?

Early November. 1-2. It's still chilly, less with each passing hour. We are not seasick. Port Said—in the evening—drizzling rain. Fosco does not want to go ashore for fear of infection. I don't want to tire D., so we don't go.

Already a week into our journey. The sea is calm. We're heading south. I am wondering about Port Said, that my parents did not want to visit. I can only draw on some vintage photographs that show rickshaws pulled by barefoot men, women in long skirts, umbrellas in hand, as if they have just stepped out of a Chekhov story; the ballroom of the Victoria hotel—now torn down—where you see musicians in tuxedos on stage, two or three small tables covered in embroidered tablecloths, and a couple of palm trees whose long fringed leaves lean toward the four stained-glass windows.

Later, in a room like that one, I would come to know through film, the Ingrid Bergman of suffused light reflected in soft eyes, of chestnut curls flickering around her neck. What enchantment binds us to an actress with a delicate smile and a crystal-clear voice? In her, I saw my young mother: the slender legs, the cut of her suit cinched at the waist, the wedge-heeled shoes. I saw her walking quickly, in a brown felt hat that partly covered her forehead, and I felt as if I were watching an entire generation of women with secret steps and sparkling eyes. Where are you going? I wanted to ask. Where are you going in such a hurry? The future has just begun. Don't hurry!

Beside her, Humphrey Bogart, trench coat slung over one shoulder, complicit cigarette between his fingers. But he was different from my father, who moved less gracefully, was more of a sportsman, more shy, more boy. The beauty of the two—diva and divo—was marvellously bound to the youth and beauty of my parents. I am there in a tableau depicting the joy of living. Could such joy ever recur?

The first taste I have known, and preserved in memory, is the taste of the voyage. The savour of just-opened luggage: mothballs, shoe polish, and perfume permeated in my mother's clothes, in which I buried my head in delight. The trunk that occupied most of the cabin opened like the chests of actors long ago: it was a true wardrobe made of a sturdy wood and lightweight, held together by strips of brass. And when we put it on end, open like a book, it served as a wardrobe with drawers that closed into the sides, and a tube across a corner for dresses and jackets on hangers. There was even room to hide behind the drawn curtain, and for the child me, a sensual refuge in the midst of the lavender scent of my mother's underwear.

On page three, here is the map that shows the route the *Conte Verde* took from Brindisi to Japan: Port Said, Aden, Bombay, Colombo, Singapore, Manila, Hong Kong, Shanghai, Tokyo, Sapporo. The painter's hand of a young adventurous mother has traced the route of the journey that will mark our lives: lines, wrinkles, curves that will brand the palm of the hand like imprints of destiny. And it's a destiny that has oriental roots.

The vessel proceeds slowly; I see it through the recollection of a mind accustomed to dreaming about books; a steamship, with its large rooms lit by glass lamps in testudo formation, fixed to the walls with metal brackets; stairways up and down, crossed by coco-mat runners; a spacious dining room where young waiters in white gloves serve dishes, legs set apart on the slippery floor, and always in motion.

Ships have remained for me a place of narrative pleasure. It's no coincidence that my first great literary loves have been novels set at sea: Stevenson and his ships that defy the mysterious underground movements of salt water, Conrad with his boats that hold inexpressible extraordinary secrets, Melville with his superhuman effort to dominate the evils of the seabed, Verne with his marvellous underwater machines. Even today, a story set at sea instantly wins me over. I am a consumer of the collections from Iperborea, the publishing house that publishes, with stubborn passion, novels about Scandinavian ghost ships, struggles with eternal ice, vessels lost in the depths of the sea, ghosts that appear in the evening along the routes of sailboats.

There's a delightful missionary on board, Father Rivelli, who is going to China. He easily befriends D., always has candy for her in his pocket, writes my mother. I don't recall this missionary, but I do know that I have never liked candy. I came to know other missionaries, especially in Africa years later, and I can say I have fallen in love with the odd wonderful white beard full of celestial solemnity, while on other occasions, I encountered little prelate hands eager for pleasure and money.

In my reawakened memory emerges an African road, a Land Rover with a broken driveshaft, and a group of us on the roadway, waiting for a ride. It was almost midnight, and we told each other stories of marauders who came out of the forest to slit the throats of tourists and to steal anything worth stealing. It was so calm all around us. We could hear crickets singing in the dark, frogs swollen with air croaking happily, certain birdcalls we imagined came from enormous birds. Everything is huge in Africa, fed by abundant waters and hothouse heat. Only the presence of the dark impenetrable forest at the side of the road caused some anxiety to the group of European travelers.

Suddenly, we hear the noise of an engine; a car approaches. Nothing less than a Mercedes, we realize as it nears, a beautiful champagne Mercedes. The car floats in a cloud of dust. When he sees us, the driver suddenly accelerates, perhaps afraid of the small band of strangers huddled at the edge of the road. But when he realizes that we are white tourists, he slows down, stops. We hasten. Inside is a bishop—small, black and elegant—with a purple sash around his waist and a giant gold ring on his finger. When we tell him our Land Rover has broken down and we don't know where to go, he waves us into the Mercedes. We squeeze together and proceed. The mission is not far, only about twenty kilometres.

We arrive at a citadel in the middle of the desert, among palms and banana trees, equipped with everything, with dozens of black servants, trucks and motorbikes parked under a straw enclosure, a number of rooms for guests, a church with a slate roof, perforated walls, and a huge ceramic crucifix.

The bishop, who knows all the soccer players on La Roma, but doesn't know Moravia or Pasolini, invites us to dinner. We eat banana porridge with meat sauce, whilst the gramophone spills out familiar music: "*Ciao ciao bambina, un bacio ancora* ...." The bishop asks about Rome, the Pope. He is cheerful, eagerly swallows his banana porridge, and lists one by one the members of his favourite team.

We sleep peacefully in wooden beds under yellow mosquito nets, under a rustling fan, in a night scented with banana and flowers—overripe succulents, whose heavy petals fall with dull thuds—in the festive barking of dogs and in the distant sound of drums.

The next morning, before leaving, we hold a secret meeting to decide how much we should leave the mission as gratitude for the hospitality. But just at that moment, the bishop's clerk arrives, dressed in black on black—very elegant—and hands us a bill. We are flabbergasted. The bishop has accounted for even the water we used for washing, and the total comes to about the price of a four-star hotel! What small offering! We pay and leave, without even seeing him, the bishop who, at ten o'clock in the morning, is still asleep.

On the other hand, I met missionary nuns who freely gave their time and energy, with touching generosity, to the sick of a small farming community in the interior of Tanzania. They hosted us for one night, because there were no hotels within a hundred miles, and I saw them hasten between the kitchen and a dirt-poor dining room to prepare a dinner worthy of the Italian guests. From them, I learned that sacrifice can also be cheerful. Catholic literature often presents sacrifice as torment, fear, sorrow, pain, mutilation, loss, suffering, sweat, and blood. Instead, the missionary nuns, affected as they were by terrible states of malaria, by chronic dysentery or filariasis (two of them had worms that entered and exited their skin like darning needles), never complained, never scowled or showed their suffering. They were so involved in the care of lepers, in the school for the poorest children, in the little hospital always short of doctors and medicine, that they had no time for themselves. And it was easier to hear them laugh and sing, instead of grumbling and complaining. As my mother says, "Humans are funny when seen from a distance, but move us when viewed closely."

Aden—I went ashore. D. remained on board with Fosco.

That's it? Is it possible that the anticipation of arrival prevented my parents from enjoying the first stop of a long exotic journey? Yet the little family was at its most joyous. Love embraced the bodies and rendered them invulnerable and eternal. My mother does not explain what she saw in Aden on that tender afternoon sixty years ago.

I have memories of Aden. Another Aden, defeated by heat, many years later. I wake up to the cry of a hyena. It's night. The air smells of cut grass. Beyond a hill, the sea breathes heavily. The meadows in front of the hostel shimmer in moonlight. I look out the window and in the suffused glow, see a group of hyenas rummaging inside plastic garbage containers. In the dark, barely illuminated by the moon, they resemble wolves. But they are easily identified by their posteriors, which are lower than their heads. This is what characterizes them. They are spotted, have pointed ears, teeth like knives, and bristly, ugly fur.

At the rustling of the raffia curtains, the beasts raise their muzzles: their eyes glitter in the dark. But they immediately understand, intelligent as they are, that I will not chase them away, that I'll simply observe them curiously. Their rummaging in the garbage raises the faint smell of rotting fruit.

Beyond them, I see a volt of vultures with long hairless necks, around the carcass of a turkey. They await their turns to plunge their beaks in the remains of the remains. Their immobile silhouettes in the light of the moon conjure silent, patient ghosts.

The heat stops me from sleeping. But if I roll up the curtains, the hyenas' cries are too close and disturbing. And what if the vultures could enter my room in one swoop through the French doors?

In embarrassment I relight the candle. In that refuge in the middle of the desert, generators are turned off at 9 p.m. I pick up the book I was reading: *Aden—Arabia*, by Paul Nizan. "I was twenty years old. I will not allow anyone to say that this is the best time of one's life. Everything is a threat to the young: love, ideas, loss of family, the entrance to adulthood. It's hard to learn one's place in the world." A blazing beginning that I quickly memorized. And now I can no longer separate the memory of the hyenas from Nizan's words. "Is this the divine harvest of literature?" said Marianna Ucria, who was a connoisseur of reading.

Bombay—we arrive around five. We can go to shore only around 11 p.m. D. is sleeping—left in the care of a waiter. We go to shore.

Fosco and Topazia, my very young parents, lovers, disembarked from the ship without me who was sleeping. I was left in the care of a waiter. I don't recall his name but I preserve in memory the warmth of his soft arms that tried to comfort me for the temporary loss of my parents. Every time they went out, I was seized by the fear that they would never return. They were too young and happy to need me. They were so in love that one did not take a step without the other. They held hands and spent the day whispering words in each other's ears, instilling in me a sense of exclusion. They laughed often, open-throated, and I wanted to laugh with them, but I did not know what they were laughing about, and this paralyzed me. Although I knew I was loved, I intuited areas of their intimacy from which I was painfully prohibited. A family, I learned at my expense, needs these spaces, while I liked to think of our little trio as compact, a body without cracks, without openings, in which everything was common and known and exchangeable.

Many years later, I went to Bombay with my partner, father, husband, and child Alberto[1] and our most tender friend Pier Paolo [Pasolini]. It was summer and the temperature rose to 45°. Our feet burned inside shoes, the air dried and scorched our nostrils, parched our lips. We could only roam the roads at five in the morning or in the evenings after nine. The rest of the day, we remained in the hotel, beneath fans circling quietly overhead, wrapped in mosquito nets, books in hand … Lying naked on top of the plaid cotton coverlets, in the lightest Madras from which shirts are made, I devoured Foster's *A Passage to India*: "The very wood seems made of mud, the inhabitants of mud moving. So abased, so monotonous is everything that meets the eye, that when the Ganges comes down it might be expected to wash the excrescence back into the soil. Houses do fall, people are drowned and left rotting, but the general outline of the town persists, swelling here, shrinking there, like some low but indestructible form of life."

---

1   Alberto Moravia, with whom Dacia lived from 1962-1978.

It's true that at times India embodies this decrepit and muddy appearance. But in its decrepitude there's something bright and astonishing. You won't need to look to the sky: "The sky settles everything—not only climates and seasons but when the earth shall be beautiful. By herself she can do little—only feeble outbursts of flowers. But when the sky chooses, glory can rain into the Chandrapore bazaars or a benediction pass from horizon to horizon. The sky can do this because it is so strong and so enormous." Under that rugged sky I saw men dressed in rags gracefully carry a dead man lying on a woven wicker stretcher. The emaciated corpse wrapped in white sheets was placed on a pile of logs to which a skeletal arm set fire with a torch. Around the dead, the relatives sat on a minuscule mat and assisted, praying at the funeral pyre. The fire crackled cheerfully, scattering a gray perfumed sandalwood cloud. Never has a funeral ceremony seemed less bleak.

Alberto and Pier Paolo had also had shirts made from pink and blue Madras cotton, shirts that we wore for years. Photos show Maria Callas, thin and melancholic: beside her, Pasolini, Moravia, or I are always wearing the Madras shirts, in a delicate light cotton that held up well in the heat. And although they had been tailored quickly, they fit us well, and even washed daily did not fade. The man who made them in Bombay was a dwarf tailor, who cut the cloth by laying it out on a long, oil-stained, wooden table, in bare feet, chewing grass that tinted his lips green.

How beautiful Maria Callas was at the peak of her artistic maturity! Blindly in love with Pier Paolo, certain to claim him, despite his homosexuality, by the force of love. She would turn her large profound eyes towards him and smile contentedly. "Mariaaaa!" he would scold her when she told bad jokes about Africa. And she would quickly go silent, mortified. She wanted to marry him and set up house with him, she told me one night when we slept together in the filthy room of a hostel, without water or light. She had had a terrible time with Onassis, who she judged rough and rude, while Pasolini she loved for his sweetness.

A woman with such an expressive explosive power became, in private, a timid naïve girl. She had a childish admiration for money and riches, as if she lived permanently inside a fairytale full of magic: a ring for her was not a ring but an object with possible extraordinary magical powers; an evening dress covered in sequins was not an expensive slightly ridiculous garment, but was there to reveal a body in love, stepping out onto the magnificent stage of the world. Her brain seemed animated only when in contact with the legendary tales of an imaginary theatre. In real life, she appeared clumsy and awkward. As if she had removed her glasses and thus lost the contour of things. "And yet, on stage," she'd say, "I was not afraid without glasses. I did a reconnaissance before I started singing and I remembered perfectly the shapes of the props. I avoided the edges, the holes, the recesses. I was marvelous!"

"And how did you manage with the conductor?"

"I couldn't see him, but it didn't matter. I could hear him. I never once missed a note," she'd say proudly. "Only once, in *Aida*, the scenographer decided at the last moment to place a pond on stage without telling me, and I went in with my dress and shoes." Her laugh was irresistible, contagious. We all laughed, imagining her there, in the middle of the stage, with her soaking feet in frigid water, yet continuing to sing like only she knew how, without missing a note, not even one …

Colombo, November 13, morning. All three of us disembark and tour around by car. I don't feel well. D. is very interested in the black black "mimmimi" and in the monkeys teeming in the public gardens. She very much enjoys feeding them peanuts.

So it really is a natural propensity we have towards animals, whose affectionate company I have enjoyed all my life: dogs always, cats sometimes, a goat, sparrows that built a nest among the books, a duck I had to give to the nuns in the countryside because she quacked early in the morning on my terrace, horses whose soft muzzle I love to caress, and whose smell never sates me, turtles, fish. If I could, I would keep an elephant and two or three giraffes. I have a good relationship with animals. I treat them as if they were people, only more innocent and lost. Someone always replies in this case: "Even the Nazis, who hated men, loved animals." And I answer that I claim the right to love animals and human beings without taking anything away from one or the other. The affection for one does not affect respect and tenderness towards the other.

Sometimes I am derided for being a vegetarian. "And the leather shoes? I don't see you wearing only cloth shoes. And the belts, the bags, are they not cowhide? So how do you reconcile this?" I admit I am a terrible vegetarian. Let's say that my refraining from meat is an act of solidarity towards mammals. Eating a cow makes much more sense to me than eating a fish. I recognize that these are sophisms. Radicalism would predicate that if one refuses to eat meat, one should refrain from eating any animal species forever, to be strictly consistent with one's choice. But getting rid of contradictions is no small feat. When I look at a poor fish with an open mouth lying on a plate, I immediately feel guilty for having inflicted its death, even though it was not me who personally did it, guilty for being about to feed on that fish. Aren't they all God's creatures? suggests a stern voice. I wonder if Saint Francis ever ate a little fish.

I remember the first sea bream I captured with a speargun while I was swimming in clear deep waters along the coasts of Ustica. One of the wildest holidays, with my father and some of his friends. Guests of a fisherman's house without running water or electricity. The long boat trips rowing until my arms ached. The songs at night on the terrace. The sea breeze. The feeds of watermelon that ended with the throwing of peels, accompanied by contagious laughter.

In the morning we dedicated ourselves to ambushes in the rocky seafloor: stones covered with algae and sea urchins, illuminated by sunrays that shattered into rhombuses, squares, soft and inconsistent circles. A strong odour of salt and rotten algae in the nostrils. I chased a seabream, moving silently among mossy boulders, the speargun pointed downwards, small waves caressing my neck, the elastic of the mask squeezing my temples, my feet lengthened and made rapid by the shiny blue fins.

The suspicious seabream had hidden in the crevices of a boulder that appeared to have rolled directly from the sky onto those clean white sands. I waited for it, knowing it would emerge to resume his hunt for the small silvery fish that moved in schools, dancing in the transparent waters. Beside my head an anemone breathed lazily, dangling its short yellow and red tentacles.

I think in that moment, I understood once and for all the sentiment of the lurking predator: a suspension between heaven and earth that makes the body feel so weightless as to forget one's mortality. A concentration that shortens the muscles as if readying to leap into a surge of animal vitality. A galvanized attention, simultaneously fierce and extremely tender, that cares for the prey, and observes it at the very moment in which it plans its destruction.

The bream came out, first shyly, only with the tip of its curved muzzle. I saw the twirl of a fearful eye and then the flicker of the tail which raised a small cloud of sand. It was trying to blur its path and it was a good move. In fact, I lost sight of it for a few moments. But its shiny back, the broad brown stripes and the extraordinary clarity of the water returned me to its tracks. Slowly, slowly, I told myself, do not make noise, do not churn the water with your flippers, do not blow into the mask's tube, breathe slowly, take a breath and prepare to attack. Is the speargun loaded? The arrow well engaged? The wrist elastic, ready to trigger the killer spring?

The performance of roles is stamped in the geography of the sky, fixed like a constellation: nothing and nobody can change it. This is the certainty of the hunter who nears its prey. The animal's task is to flee, to hide, to pretend to sidestep the enemy, to raise dust, to turn abruptly on itself. The hunter's task is to chase him, flush him out, reach him and hit him. There is no possibility of reversing the parts. Yes they are there, fixed for eternity. So thinks the hunter as he aims patiently at the escaping animal. And immediately I am reminded of the girl I once was, blonde and thin, with her scraped knees, who moved with careless trust in the lustrous waters of post-war Sicily.

A hunter sees me, decides to go hunting. He chases me, he teases me with kind words. He aims. And because I'm much less suspicious than the bream, and the hunter in question is a dear friend of the family, I approach him, smiling and am hit by a poisoned arrow that does not kill me but wounds me irreparably for the future. The scar will never disappear.

Is this a question of point of view? Or is there in some part of consciousness a feeling of fairness through which the predator and the prey recognize each other and decide not to play that game of waiting and horror anymore? Maybe if we stopped pursuing and catching each other, we would make the sky fall.

Nature, or God, created carnivorous men, created hunters, many say, in the sublime presumption that the human race is superior to any other living being on earth. But, but … the doubts are many and are born the moment that science discovers, almost against its own will, a complex and varied animal world, in which intelligence and the capacity to communicate are daily found to be bolder and more imaginative. As well, as Dr. Umberto Veronesi—a vegetarian—says, we are descended from primates and primates did not eat meat.

To ease our peace of mind regarding those wonderful cows with mild and gentle eyes, endowed with maternal and paternal feelings, we have thought it convenient to believe that they have no thoughts and above all no affection. But science tells us that what animals feel when faced with pain, both physical and moral, is not so different from what we feel. The thoughts of donkeys, of horses, of goats are perhaps more inarticulate, but they exist and understand defence mechanisms, strategies for survival, curious methods of adaptation to the most brutal slavery, so as not to go extinct. How can we not take this into account?

The blonde girl at this point has pierced the body of the bream from one side to the other with a metal spear with articulated wings. Now she pulls up, levering her flippers against the water in a fast pedal, the string that ties the spear to the speargun. A moment later she grasps the bream that flounders in her hand searching oxygen while its blood flows between her fingers and disperses in the transparent water bathed in sunlight.

The blonde girl observes that blood that melts and flows away, observes the fish in its ultimate agony, observes the round eyes now spent, and she is horrified with herself. In that moment, the hunter recuperates the ability to split herself, to identify and become prey. Why, she hears herself questioned by an inner voice, inopportune but insistent, why did you do this? Why? That bream, it's pointless to say, I was not able to eat.

From that day on, I have never hunted with a speargun. I limited myself to observing fish swim cautiously and quickly, without being overcome by the need to flush them out and kill them. And I matured into thinking that while hunting is exciting, it's too unfair and useless in a world that already enslaves animals. Once the hunt corresponded to some reciprocity: the man armed with a rifle in a hostile forest faced herds of animals that would have torn him limb from limb. But now, to what has the hunt been reduced? An organized game, where one pays money in which poor animals are thrown into an arena in order to be shot by wealthy hunters, or to a farce in which a man with increasingly sophisticated and deadly weapons takes it out on birds he won't even eat, for the sheer pleasure of shooting and killing.

Singapore. Again, all three of us disembark. Then: Singapore— Manilla—a rough sea. I begin to suffer more. D. left more and more with ... the waiters! Who love her!

I wonder why these waiters adored me. Could this be the illusion of a loving mother? Or maybe they stayed around me because I amused them with my shenanigans. Back then, I thought instinctively that adults were to be entertained and amused, otherwise who knows what they would have done to me. Or maybe they adored me because I listened to them. My natural instinct has always been to be a patient, avid listener, the carnal recipient of the most bizarre and unhappy stories, the most varied and joyful ones. As I grew, I became the gatherer of stories, and I never tire of hearing them. People understand this and confide in me their most hidden and complicated truths.

Singapore, my mother writes, in a hurried hand, the hand of a scrupulous young bride, but also one impatient to reach her destination. And yet, Singapore must have been a surprising novelty for her too. Who knows what we visited when we left the ship ... the history museum? The ancient quarter? Of antiquity real and proper, however we cannot speak: Singapore was born as a commercial trading post in 1819 [British East India Company], founded by Lieutenant Sir Stamford Raffles, who formed an alliance with a local leader, Temenggong Abdul Rahman. So the history books say. Scores of Chinese were the first to arrive and, uniting with the women of the Peninsula of Malacca, gave life to a population that was called Peranakani, or Baba.

Perhaps my two very young parents—lovers—boarded a waterbus to the foot of Faber mountain to go to the island of Sentosa to see a pirates' cemetery. Or maybe they visited the Moschea, constructed in the 1800s by the last sultan of Singapore, Iskandar Shah. Or they may have gone to search the famous hydroponics: there, where earth is scarce, and the population overly abundant, farmers seed lettuce and turnips directly in water.

It's a pity my mother didn't recount the Singapore of those days: a city of narrow crowded streets, the street vendors with their hand carts, the panting rickshaw drivers, the cloth dyers hanging fabrics dripping red and purple onto the bushes of the public gardens, the dust that swirls day and night along the unpaved roads, the monkeys that leap roof to roof, stealing fruits hung out to dry.

I have never been back to Singapore, having lost the joy of travelling by sea. Even if I wanted to, there are no longer any passenger vessels. But I have often flown over it. Besides, I have encountered it, before it even existed as a city, in the form of the mysterious

Malaysian lands that surround it, inside the books of beloved writers. The azure hills of Conrad, the petrified forests of Stevenson, the impetuous rivers of Jules Verne, the mysterious cities of Green.

Today I know that like Beijing, like Seoul, like Shanghai, Singapore, too, has become an enormous cement box, with skyscrapers hundreds of metres high, beside small houses with terra cotta shingles, the streets invaded by a river of American and Japanese automobiles.

What remains is the Singapore of American films that so fascinated me when I was a child. I remember one with Ava Gardner and Fred McMurray, she, beautiful, dark, who moved like a boa constrictor. I don't remember hardly anything of the story but I know there were many young women with wasp waists and many roguish young men. I think it's about a Marine, who retraces his steps to a recent war, of a meeting, of a dangerous love.

Once in a Roman restaurant I saw coming towards me a tall splendid woman dressed dark as night, her smile a crescent moon. It was her, Ava Gardner. I heard her laugh and I saw her take the arm of a lanky lighthearted young man. She called him Walter. I was a little girl who was enchanted by cinema; they were the divinity of a sky made of stars, who wore floppy hats, curls at their necks, and makeup on their eyes. Yankee, Yankee, doodle doo …

Manila—Hong Kong. The sea rough. I have to stay in bed. At certain moments, Fosco too can't take it. One evening—the worst—in the dining room there was no one. Only D. seated by herself at a large table, magnificently eating every sort of delicacy, surrounded by the entire group of layabout waiters. I happened to see her while I moved from the bridge to the … bed.

At this point I ask myself: when did I begin to suffer from seasickness? How is it that today just standing on the waiting docks of the vaporetti in Venice makes me nauseous. When did the flaxen haired girl transform herself from a strong sea-fearer, master of all the ships, into a timid young woman with a stomach always in turmoil?

In my furthest memories the sea under my feet seems an enemy, a harbinger of seasickness. How come I was immune at two? Is seasickness something you learn, a kind of cultural heritage received as a dowry through maternal kindness, after the age of three, five years?

Hong Kong. Beautiful. We toured around for some hours by car—always with Daciuzza. D.'s little friend, Lilongo Tam, disembarked and is remaining here. They were a very nice family.

Of that stop in Hong Kong there are only these few words. I returned years later with Alberto, hosted by a lovely family of doctors, who kept two chimpanzees on the top floor, and three white and red parrots in the basement, chained to high perches. I quickly made friends with one of the chimpanzees, and carried him with me during a long boat ride in the bay. I still have a photograph of that excursion with the chimpanzee in my arms. Was I miming, perhaps, the tenderness of a brutally interrupted maternity? I had lost a child a couple of years earlier, in the seventh month. With that child went all the allure of a family I had imagined I would nurture and tend to. My young husband, Lucio, disillusioned, had gone to New York to build a new family. A wife "who looks a lot like you" as my mother-in-law said, with whom he had three children. Whom later he divorced then married a much younger woman, who gave him another child. The handsome Lucino has lost his hair, his face is full of wrinkles, but he has a young man's timid, athletic body, bright eyes, and the sweetest smile. When I go to New York, I phone him and he invites me to his studio that smells of turpentine, and shows me his latest massive paintings on which writhe larval bodies and obsessive mysterious figures.

Another time I landed in Hong Kong on a stopover, during a flight to Australia, where one of my plays was being performed. The plane landed in the middle of wind gusts, on a narrow strip between skyscrapers and sea. It was like sliding the entire airplane into a box.

Only a few centimetres of error would have sheared off the plane's casing and plunged us into the ocean.

The plane had to land quickly on that scrap of runway because it was racing a hurricane. The sky was leaden, the sea furrowed with long blackish bands. Scraps of paper, rags and even steel signs spun in the streets. In the port, the many families who live on boats were chasing household goods below deck, pulling down ropes of laundry hung out to dry, tying the poor furnishings with ropes and strings. The hurricane would have spared no one. In fact, a few hours later it exploded with a fury that we Mediterraneans know nothing about. From the window of the hotel in which it was prohibited to exit, I witnessed the growing anger of the sea. The waves rose higher and higher, the salt water clambered up to the ramps of the port, then flung itself angrily along the streets, crashing into and flooding houses and shops. I saw people running in bare legs, searching for refuge in doorways, dragging behind them large bundles laden with fluttering hens, trembling pigs, and even crying babies. The next day it seemed that a war had passed through the streets: trees upended, shop windows shattered, torn awnings, overturned cars, wood and brick debris piled in the middle of the streets. But the people did not seem desperate. With an ancient patience that testifies to the frequency of these shocks, they cheerfully began to remedy the damage. The floating houses hung wet laundry out to dry, in the evening paper lanterns reappeared on poles, tricycles started running again and the shops reopened their shutters after tons of stinking mud were unloaded onto the roadside.

24 November Shanghai. Where we will stay for a week.

It was a much more human way to travel than today. We approached a destination slowly, stopping to reflect, to enjoy the stops along the way. There was time to savour the new country, to understand the distances, to dream of the future, while lulled by the waves.

Many invitations—much to do—people to see, continues my mother and it's difficult for me to understand who these people

were. How could they know so many people if they had just disembarked and would depart in a week?

Then there was the girl: who would take care of her? *We will
leave D. at the Hotel with a "hama,"* continues my mother, *they sent
me one who is very pretty and clean—she wears dark blue pants under a
white apron, her shiny hair is the blackest black, and tightly knotted and
tied back. Many gold teeth. Golden skin. She has a sharp smell—but not
of dirt and not disagreeable. D. detests staying with her, but as soon as
we leave, she is happy to play with her.*

The art of settling down. That I had to learn early, with two
parents who were far from being inclined to spoil me.

In my mother I perceive a secure sense of class when speaking of nannies, of maids, of housekeepers, as if they were a natural
attribute of the family. In this, we can discern the passage from
one generation to the next. For me it is almost improper to pay a
woman to clean and iron my clothes when I can do it myself. "Don't
be a Jacobin! The world is made like this, and you can't change it."
I know. But I cannot prevent another seed from being thrown into
the meadow of my consciousness, where the grasses of reproach
proliferate.

*Every now and then I take D. out in a rickshaw. She likes it immensely—
would never get down. Naturally like in the hotel, outside she is admired
by everyone. Perhaps it's because she is blonde and independent. Along
the streets, she trots by herself in front of me. She won't let me hold her
hand, and when we approach main streets crowded with Chinese people,
I worry about animal infections, shoving … […] So we take refuge in a
rickshaw—but it's good to walk a bit!*

My poor mother, split between wanting to take a walk and being
afraid that her child will be trampled!

In September 2000, I was in China for the publication of my
new novel. I saw a city transformed in monsters of cement and
glass: the buildings rise arrogantly towards the sky, huge glitter-
ing banks have forced out the fruit and vegetable shops, cars have

replaced the bicycles. And yet, I found the rickshaw of my mother, slipping dangerously in the midst of metallic traffic. A poor ramshackle cart hitched to a bicycle, pedalled by a young man in a tank top. The only evidence of a China now gone. Humble anachronistic human machines that, despite the banks, despite the supermarkets, despite the infinite cars, continue to pedal with bare feet cinched into plastic sandals, laboriously leveraging the lean muscles of their legs to earn some money along the wide avenues of Beijing.

Shanghai—Kobe. On the English steamer Corfu. It is terrible compared to the Conte Verde. You eat badly and you have to precisely adhere to time. And I always feel somewhat ill.

So we have changed ships. And here, in the midst of the British, one has to conform to tight rules. The sea evidently is often rough, and my mother is suffering from nausea. It's assumed that the child is well. In fact, after a while, my mother writes:

D. always loves to walk around alone and would like to climb everywhere. The stair of the last bridge is her favourite, it's like a trapeze—up and down until she tires. I have to look out for her without helping her or she protests energetically.

Notes on the character of her daughter by a careful observer. My mother studied and judged me, putting aside her impetuous maternal love to understand the defects, the qualities of a child who would become a girl and then a woman. She studied me unscrupulously. And she found me proud beyond all limits, and stubborn too. In fact, I have always been stubborn. I don't know if in this I take more after my father or my mother. Both of them are absolutely determined when they decide to dedicate themselves to a cause they believe is just. On the other hand: from whom would I have gotten this spirit of independence and resolve if not from her and her beloved husband who became my father?

"I hear your pride when you talk about your stubbornness," said a Sicilian friend of mine, always very critical of me. This book, I'm certain, he would find "disgustingly narcissistic," not knowing that it grew out of the discovery of my mother's journals. To which I should only have added a preface. But when I began to write, my hand continued and wouldn't stop. Writers, it's true, are often immodest. Of their lives they construct narratives, and they cannot refrain from chasing characters from their own past with comic and naïve determination, and who knows, maybe even with some blatant and reprehensible narcissism.

"You have a morbid and disturbing propensity towards the recovery of dead and buried things. I don't think it's good for your health," my friend would insist, who the crueler he gets, the more affectionate and smiling he becomes.

"Stubbornness," my grandfather Antonio called his wife Yoi, reproaching her for not knowing how to approach the thoughts of others. Something that not even he could do. Despite his affability, despite his extreme courtesy, one could feel in his manners an utterly diplomatic, icy affectation. When he was generous, he had a strategy in mind. And both my father and grandmother Yoi secretly opposed these calculating amiabilities. He was a composed and courteous man inhabited by a severe censor, who observed him and made pungent judgments but, before declaring them, he looked around considering the forces at play. Never a false move.

Early in the morning, he would stoop to nurture the dahlias with their languid, marvellous colours. In the last years of his life, he devoted himself entirely to the garden of Terra du Sopra. This is how I remember him, curved over his flowers, dressed all in white, wearing a straw hat. Grandmother was dead. He nurtured those dahlias with a paternal devotion, breaking off dead leaves, cleaning insects off the petals, showering them in a veil of water, feeding them with fertilizer. He would raise his head when I arrived, breathless from running up the stairs of the garden.

I arrived home from school on Sundays, and I wanted to get out and sunbathe. But as soon as I came in contact with his inquisitive gaze, I composed myself. I saw that he was studying me, perhaps with affection, but without indulgence, looking for failure. And finding it, naturally, because I was a young woman always in motion, impetuous and looking for trouble. "It's true, maybe you do resemble your grandmother Yoi a bit, but she was good and you're not," he'd say in a calm, punitive voice. What bad had I done? Guilt was already clinging to my spine. "You stole cherries from the tree, you soiled your dress, your grandmother would never have done that, even when she was five."

Another time at a dinner table in Florence he said, "You might have your Nonna Yoi's eyes, but she was beautiful and you're not." Then seeing my mortified face, he continued, "She didn't have the Mongolian fold[2] you and Fosco have." But where had my father's Mongolian fold come from, if not from him?

Like the Mongolian fold, he always found something that prevented me from reaching my grandmother's standard, who also looked like me according to everyone. He gloated, I could see it, like an old turkey when he managed to hurt me.

I ask myself whether I'm simply reflecting the memory of my father's dislike for him ... they never got along, Grandfather and Papà. They never understood nor were tender toward each other. My father was a strange creature, as if born only from his mother without the intervention of his father, so it seemed my grandfather thought. Even if he looked like him, in his smile in the cut of his eyes, in the strong small hands. They did not recognize each other as father and son, and from that much trouble was born. Certainly the trip to Japan was above all my father's escape from his physical father and his political father, who in that moment was raging from the balcony of Piazza Venezia and demanded obedience and dedication. I can't say if this voluntary exile was all negative. Certainly, if we had remained in Italy we would not have ended up in a concentration camp for anti-fascists in Nagoya.

A fate of desertion born from a resolute stubbornness for which the father reproached the son, attributing it to his mother, and that the son had endured for too long, and in turn had blamed his father, despite their clever strategies of peace. "My father, I

---

2   Epicanthic fold.

wish that you and I / in a cool grave dripping with water / I wish that we, but your face / my father, blue and hardened, between thin eyebrows / and convex brow, between curled lips / and sharp chin / in a sunny valley / I wish that you and I, my father / could tell each other the truth ..." I wrote in 1966 in *Crudeltà all'aria aperta*. (*Cruelty in open air*)

Kobe 1° December 1938. Only for an afternoon. Touring around with D. who is not calm enough to want to sleep in the afternoon. This unsettled life is not good for a little girl. I can't wait till we arrive at our destination. All three of us are tired and our trunks are in a dishevelled state.

In front of me I have a postcard of the Ikuta Shrine, the temple with the wooden points reaching for the sky, dedicated to the goddess Wakahirume-no-Miloto, who they say is the sister of the great goddess Amaterasu Omikami. Only a few Japanese cedars and a camphor tree here and there, evidence of the immense park that surrounded the small port. The cedars and camphor were cut in the nineteenth century to make room for the massive frame of the station of Sannomiya. On one side rises the strange monument in Oriental style dedicated to the French astronomer P.J.C. Janssen, who apparently was in Kobe in 1874 to observe the passage of Venus in the Japanese sky. I wonder if my young parents found a way to climb the mountain that overlooks the city to reach the Buddhist temple Dairyuji, founded in 768 by Wake-no-Kiyomaro "the most loyal of nobles of the Nara court." And who knows whether they were able to see the lacquered wooden statue of Nyoirin Kannon, sculpted in 710. Here it seems, Kobo Daishi introduced the Shingon doctrine in the beginning of the ninth century, having returned from China where he had gone to study Buddhism. Who knows if the European shoes of Fosco and Top (as my father called my mother) stopped on the meadow that circled that famous stone monument under which was written: "Ah, here lies the faithful Kusunoki." But who was Kusunoki? I who love stories, always find someone who tells me.

Kusunoki Masashige was a famous warrior who, in the name of the emperor, stood up to an army of thousands of men led by Ashikaga Takauji, the rebel. It was May of 1336. After hours of battle, Takauji prevailed, and Kusunoki Masashige, with his 700 men loyal to the sovereign, was forced to withdraw. From that moment on, either he surrendered to the enemy (both his and the emperor's) or he had to commit hara-kiri. He chose to slice open his belly with a sharp blade while a companion-in-arms severed his head. After him, all 700 warriors loyal to the emperor committed hara-kiri. This is what Japan is. Ah, here lies the loyal Kusunoki!

Everything—the trees, the statues, the temples, the cases, the monuments, the gardens—was demolished in the bombing of the Second World War. Reconstructed with the proverbial patience of the Japanese, it was again destroyed by the blind fury of the devastating earthquake of 1995. Poor Kobe! I wish that in the distant secret memory of my childhood eyes there could have remained some fragment, some small image of Kobe before the war, before the earthquake, like an infantile dream impossible to obliterate: the twisted graceful branch of a cedar with almost white leaves; two tufts of Camphor flowers, yellow and with a strong pungent smell, a wooden arm of Buddha, lacquered red, a stone hand of the French astronomer Janssen who holds a pair of binoculars from which one can still see a bright and weeping Venus.

I tear myself away from that imaginary Kobe to return to the voyage towards the Sapporo of many years ago. And yet that feeling of suspension between one place and another, beside cluttered suitcases, is so familiar that I have never freed myself from it. So many cities, so many houses that I have loved but have always lost. Nomadism is a torrent that flows in family veins and I don't think I can ever really stop without planning a voyage soon after.

Kobe—Tokyo. At first, D. amuses herself, then naturally, she tires because she doesn't know what to do. She tires of the few toys at her disposal—she dirties her hands, her face, her legs and we don't have enough clothes.

Another train, another journey, another landscape. And the small blonde girl can't sit still. She looks out the window and contemplates the endless rice fields that extend, one after the other, along the railway. She sits down to read a book while still not being able to distinguish the words on the page. She sings the Pinocchio song with her mother. She sleeps a little with her head in her mother's lap. But certainly she is bored. Because at this point, she would like a house, a real bed, a garden in which to run. The nomadism of the family is mitigated by the certainty of the return. One departs in order to return. One dreams in order to awaken. One craves night in order to dream.

Finally we arrive in Tokyo. The first landing: Imperial Hotel. A large building, a rational design by Frank Lloyd Wright. One of the few hotels that will not crumble in the tempest of bombs of the last war. Instead, however, it will be razed to the ground in the aftermath of war by the eager, reckless "innovators," who construct in its place a brand new hotel and of the old keep only its name.

In the 70s, I returned to Tokyo. It was the same place, but there was nothing left of the genius of Wright: of those vaulted corridors that had withstood earthquakes and bombs, of those large halls with bell-shaped ceilings, not even a shadow. In their place, halls of polished marble, double-paned windows framed in gold; in other words, a normal luxury hotel of the 1950s. At the Imperial Hotel, we didn't stay long also because it was very expensive. We quickly found refuge in the Bunka apartments. *There are many people to see,* my mother comments, *innumerable invitations, from every member of the embassy. I explained that I can't leave D. alone. They all want us to take her with us, and so she is present at all the dinners and breakfasts. She doesn't want to leave me for a moment. It seems that the voyage has made her nervous. It is difficult not to upset her and at the same time to not encourage bad habits.*

Here too it's cold. I have a cold. Dacia no.

All the Japanese are very kind—even too much—with children and with D. it seems in a special way.

It's strange to feel ourselves so scrutinized. The crowded Ginza avenue is D.'s battlefield, and she is a watershed between the skirts (kimonos) and the clogs, to collect a trail of "kamai né?" (cute, eh?). It's almost embarrassing. They smile at me and I feel like those royals who pass between two lines of citizens who are forced to smile and bow.

At that time it was so rare to see strangers, that a blonde child was a sensation. Today no one would turn to look at a little girl who doesn't have black hair cut in a pageboy, narrow almond-shaped eyes, and a snub nose. Had I perhaps, learned the feeling of being different? Children do not want to be different from their peers. In fact I wanted to have black hair, and not blonde ones like cornbread; I would've liked to have olive skin not one white one as mozzarella. I would've liked a pair of black eyes, cut elegantly, with a more accentuated Mongoloid fold, despite the contempt of my grandfather Antonio. But back then I didn't know him and I didn't know that he would have a particular antipathy for the Mongoloid fold he criticized in his son as if it were a character defect.

Tokyo—Hakodate—SAPPORO. The voyage tiring, long. I think that D. is relatively very good. She wants to travel far and wide throughout the compartment and stops without shyness in front of people of all kinds and soldiers and officers in particular.

On the steamer from Aomori to Hakodate we have breakfast at the same table as four officers. D. climbs in turn on the laps of everyone, who embrace her, swing her, and play with her like children with a doll!

This propensity for officials is curious. I wouldn't have imagined this. The propensity of the officials for dolls instead is a little more predictable. It's possible that for children the uniform makes a particular impression. Is it possible that what attracts them is a sense of authority that uniforms possess? But why would children be attracted by authority? Perhaps because they are escaping from the disorder in which they were immersed before they were born? Or perhaps because they feel the distinct darkness from which they came always dangerously near? Is birth not also a passage from the chaos of matter to the need to order and catalogue things through the attribution of names? How to own those objects that present themselves to us full of surprises and of promises without the help of language? Perhaps a uniform is a primal form of language, clear and consequent, that even a feral child can understand.

From Hakodate to Sapporo they gave us a luxurious compartment all to ourselves—it's much more comfortable for D. who has more space to climb up and down and lie down on the seats.

At the restaurant car a fat man from the bottom of the compart- ment sends a plate of sweets and chocolates to D. Fosco and I are al little confused. Another, after a while, sends fruit and torrone. We are truly overwhelmed and D. very naturally smiles and gives thanks, accepting all as if it were owed!

Clearly, they were spoiling me, both my parents and strangers. But who wanted to make me feel different and special if not her, a vir- tuous woman, so happy with this little girl as to have reigned her queen before she even had teeth?

SAPPORO. 15 December 1938. They expect us at the Grand Hotel. The city at night—with few lights, some of which are coloured, that reflect on the substantial snow—seems like a scene from Christmas night.

In the morning I go out with D. Everyone turns to look at her with the usual exclamations of "kawai kawai." The people here are kind and different from those in Tokyo. I like the atmosphere immediately. One of the things that impresses D. is the large number of crows that jump heavily from tree to tree with loud "qua qua qua qua."

I don't know if it was really during that time, but my mother sang to me for the first time an old popular song, "O dearest little girls come here, to hear the story of the crow of Canada." I remember her fluid, voice that never sated me. "Again, Mamà ..."

And she would continue, "One day, a female crow stood on a lawn and a male crow winked at her from the window." But soon, she would become distracted.

"Again, Mamà ..."

And she would continue, "But the lovely female crow didn't care about that love, because under the grass was the sniper Cecchino ... Is that enough?"

"No. Tell me the ending."

"I don't remember it." It wasn't true, in reality she didn't perhaps want me to participate in a cruel conclusion. "I beg you ... I don't remember ..."

"Then begin at the beginning."

And she would patiently repeat: "O dearest little girls, come here, to hear the story of the crow of Canada." But I knew how it would end.

It was a song that amazed and intrigued me: how can you fall in love with your assassin? It seemed to me an unnatural thing that that crow fluttered around Cecchino's rifle knowing that he would fire. Perhaps it was just this that attracted me. Years later I learned that in effect many women, from old habits of suggestion, often fall in love with Cecchino, the courteous sniper who, as the song says, in the end vents his predatory instinct, "Boom, he shot and killed it."

All the women who open doors to their own assassins, and there are many, are they not unwittingly in love with Cecchino? But Cecchino with his indolent airs, his bronze face, his fascinating blond tuft, often does not understand the love that worries and annoys him, to the point, sometimes, of wielding the rifle.

We begin the search for a house. The university has a perfect one available in a row of professor residences.

Professor Kodama introduces us to our future neighbors—Hecker and Lane. This will be our house for about two years. I absolutely want it to be clean and ready for Christmas. I need electricians, window clean-ers, plumbers, heating contractors, etc.

Here my mother rolled up her sleeves, exactly like two centuries earlier her great grandmother Marianna had done (my mother's second name is also Marianna) to make up for the inertia or absence of her husband and build a house for herself and her children. When I wrote of Marianna in the Sicilian novel, I was thinking of my mother, so active and determined, used to doing everything by herself, and often taking on unsuitable burdens.

A little ant with a solid thought for the future, my sober and hardworking mom. She was nothing like Grandmother Sonia, who was instead a cicada. She even had the powerful, tireless voice of a cicada. She liked to sing on the perfumed branch of a cherry tree, while the fruit went from white and hard, to pink and soft, then to red and shiny. But at a certain point, *splat*, promptly the fruit would end up in the belly of an enterprising bird. Grandmother Sonia sang all her life, saved nothing. She died—with the key of the safe attached to her wrist—she had given away all her prop-erty in exchange for a pension. In the safe she kept fake gems. Costume jewellery. For my wedding with Lucio, which occurred in Rome, she sent a beautiful box inside of which lay a diamond necklace, accompanied by a note full of compliments and at the end she added, "After you've shown this to your future in-laws, send me back the necklace because I want to keep it." Scrupulous grandchild that I am I sent it back to her, careful to not lose even one precious stone. To discover, after her death, that they were fake diamonds. The real ones she had sold in one of her most vocal summers of song.

We enter our new house on the 22nd. Hecker [...] sends sweets and bottles of wonderful things—flowers and mandarins.

[...] Wool tablecloths, cups, tray.

We are confused. These people are so extremely courteous and wel-coming that we are almost dismayed.

We send Italian vermouth and baskets of fruit—games for the Lane children.

A good initiation to the "culture of giving." One gives to prepare alliances, to create obligations, to celebrate each other, to appease any aggression and competition. Which goes to show that Japan is a highly competitive, highly authoritarian country. With a deep enduring love for gifts and celebratory ceremonies.

For them any occasion is a good occasion to bring gifts. Not only to celebrate the birth of a prophet, as happens for us, recalling the three magi which arrive from distant lands with myrrh and incense for the baby Christ, even if he was born in a stall. The Japanese bring offerings to all social locations: a dinner, a drive, a meeting with the teacher at school, the beginning of a work collaboration, the welcoming to a stranger, and so on. And in the language of gifts, the offering is meant to calm, to appease, to quell a frowning god who could annihilate us. Even the ancients did the same. But their offerings to the gods had to be accompanied by innocent blood. Then, with time, the sacrifices became less bloody, have become purely symbolic. What remains is the intention of placating the ire of distant, capricious, unpredictable gods who could unleash themselves against us.

The powerful ceremony, however, has now been reduced to a vague and poetic exchange of trinkets, valueless objects, small smooth boxes of rice cakes. It's no accident that the art of packaging is very refined in Japan, I would say even sublime. One is amazed and enchanted to watch the small fingers of a saleswoman who folds the paper so that, without making folds, it fits perfectly on the object in question to deliver it, squared, flattened, bowed, into the hands of the buyer. And here, with that pleasure of connections that are typical of those who love to read, the words of Pirandello in his *The Man With the Flower in His Mouth* come to mind, when he who is waiting for the train with packages in his arms relates the skill of a salesman, "What hands! A nice big sheet of 2-ply paper, red, flawless ... It's a pleasure to see it ... So smooth that one could put one's face in it to feel the fresh caress ... He spreads it on the counter and then with graceful ease places on it, in the middle, the light, well-folded cloth. First he lifts a flap from the bottom with the back of his hand; then, from above, he lowers the other flap and makes an extra tuck, as a plus for the love of art; then he folds from one side to the other in a triangle and catches the two points under it; he reaches out to the twine box; pulls just enough to tie the bundle; and ties it so quickly, that you don't even have time to admire his skill—you can already see the package with the noose ready to introduce your finger ..."

We decorated a magnificent Christmas tree. Last year also D. trimmed two of them (one here and one with her grandma Yoi) but this year she's older and enjoying it more. All she wants to do is play with the decorations and she jumps on chairs in order to reach them and take them from the tree.

An endearing action: to stand on a chair and hang silver balls on the branches. I watched my mother do it many times and I repeat it, even without children, enjoying the traces of a distant carefree act. Since then I've always loved decorating and taking down the Christmas tree. In my house in the mountains, in the Abruzzi park, each year I buy a Christmas tree. "But I want one with roots," I say and almost always I bring home a little fir, with its roots well wrapped in burlap, that after the holidays, I plant in my garden. Almost all of them have taken, and it's a pleasure for me to observe how they grow, how they fill with buds during the summer months. Some have died, but certainly it was because the roots were cut too drastically.

I like a Christmas tree to be monochromatic. I hang the lightest silver balls, enliven it with iridescent garlands of tinsel. On top, I place a comet. I don't have children in the house who can enjoy the ornaments, but I have many friends who visit during the holidays. We converse, cook, read aloud, dance, and walk through the woods. On Christmas eve, I prepare fish. And I spend hours packing gifts of all kinds: many books, slippers (in my house we wear slippers to avoid the mud and the imprints of runners necessary for walks), coloured blankets, delicious honey of acacia, eucalyptus, chestnut, thyme. I'm not as good as the Japanese shop assistants, but my packages have a certain elegance that I'm proud of. The gift-giving culture continues to produce its effects. But which frowning God am I trying to placate?

It was a wooden house, the one in Sapporo, made of that pale pine. In the middle of a minuscule garden, where in the summer grew elderberries, whose white flowers around September were transformed into clusters of black violet fruit ... in this house my memories take form with a certain frequency. I'm almost three years old and the first huge emotions come with snow. Flakes that fall slowly already in October and continue to fall until May, creating chasms of silence. The muffled silence of the trees, the dampened silence of the streets, broken only now and then by the dull thuds of snow accumulated along the roofs that fall onto the sidewalk. I slept curled up in my bed in a wooden room that smelled of smoke and soy, my ears listening to the light sounds of night that never seemed to end.

I was beginning my first confused reflections on eternity, that later I would continue: according to my childish logic, it would have been a long day without me, a serene and relaxed time, absolutely indifferent to my small mental precipices. A time outside my body; very difficult to imagine. Was eternity death? And yet the Japanese girls recited by memory the rules of reincarnation: one was reborn after death, even ten, twenty times, depending on the worth and their passions. My father did not believe in this and neither did my mother. How could they trust the seductive thought of continual rebirth?

I would fall asleep at the beginning of dawn and I would awaken a few hours later, sleepy. From the scents of coffee and porridge that came from the kitchen, I understood that my mother was already up. Our porridge habit came from Nonna Yoi who had brought

British customs of boiled oats to Florence. The hot, flaky, soggy and tasteless mush was covered with cold milk and sugar. I was so accustomed to that taste that a morning without porridge would've seemed to be a morning without awakening. It took the concentration camp to break this delicious Anglo Florentine custom.

Nonna Yoi, how sad that I didn't get to know her better. A great traveller who was inspired by Ruskin's *The Stones of Venice* and *The Seven Lamps of Architecture*, she surrounded herself with precious objects and Oriental fabrics. It seems that Ruskin was a difficult man, grudging and miserly in everyday life, vacillating between periods of excitement and periods of delusional depression. In London, in the winter of 2000, I saw a provocative show of Ruskin's life, the European idol of the first half of the 20th Century, beloved the world over for his studies on architecture and painting, for his understanding the rapport between art and the society that expresses it, for his invectives against mercantilism, his passion for the gothic and for beautiful bold and elegant writing.

This extremely intelligent scholar seems to have been so sarcastic and cruel to his wife Eufemia Gray, called Effie, that he angrily pushed her into the arms of his best pupil John Everett Millais. Caught between a non-declared homosexuality, the obsessive and morbid love for his tyrannical mother, and the desire for normalcy that rendered him mad and ferocious, Ruskin dedicated himself more and more to stones and to devotion for the magnificent painter Turner.

My adorable grandmother Yoi, who I will never be fortunate enough to spend time with, because I left Italy when I was two, and when I returned, she was gone … A woman whose extraordinary stories we told in the family, even if they were vaguely disturbing. Was it true that she had abandoned a husband and two children to go travelling alone at the beginning of the 20th century? Was it true that she became infatuated with an Persian poet, and followed him to Baghdad? Was it true that from Baghdad she left, alone, and landed in Florence where she fell in love with the sculptor, my grandfather Antonio, 10 years her junior, and went to live with him in a farmhouse in Poggio Imperiale? Was it true that her children from her first marriage continued to love her, and every now and then came to visit her from cold England?

I first knew her through the photograph in the living room at Torre di Sopra, which showed her covered in wrinkles, her hair like a donut around a perfect oval. Many years after her death, I don't know how, but in my sister Yuki's house there appeared an extraordinary oil painting of her in youth, closed like a tuberose inside a dress of light lace, delicate and elegant. Slender articulated arms, the very long neck, almond-shaped eyes my father inherited, notwithstanding Grandfather Antonio's malicious fantasies on the Mongolian fold, the full and sensual mouth.

Grandmother Yoi's writing in her novels was both sweet and ironic. Her travel descriptions were inspired by the great books of travellers of the 18th century. But she certainly must have read and loved Flaubert, Lamartine, Merimée, and Madame de Sévigné, from which she had drawn irony, detachment and a kind and bold way of observing the world. She had a secular aesthetic view of her contemporaries. A poetic sensibility, sorrowful and floral when describing nature. She paid maternal attention to and supported the poor, the excluded; she was cultured and smiling. She loved to surround herself with cushions and curtains of Indian cloth, of exotic necklaces and bracelets, of refined Chinese objects. Of hers I still have a tortoise shell toilette set with her name inscribed in gold. A brush, a rectangular box, a powder box (compact), a framed mirror, a small clock. She was a contemporary of Virginia Woolf and in some way shared her ideals: she defended tooth and nail her freedom as emancipated woman; she looked with a certain haughtiness at the world of men, who claimed to demonstrate the superiority of one race over another; she was a friend of Berenson, loved Ming pottery and the music of Debussy, the paintings of Kandinskij, and certainly she felt much affinity with her most sensitive and bizarre contemporary, the man with the fluid memory who was Marcel Proust.

On the day of the death of his mother during the war, while we were imprisoned in a concentration camp and had not had news from Italy for a year, my father felt a mysterious pang that left him breathless and with a great desire to cry. Only after almost two years, returning to Florence, he reconstructed that it had happened exactly on the day that his mother died. Grandmother was in the garden, at least this is what Grandfather told us. "Antonio! Antonio!" He had rushed out and had found her on the ground, lifeless.

I would like to die like this too, in the open air. I hate hospitals, the beds, the oxygen tubes, the smell of disinfectant that impregnates every object.

Grandfather Antonio instead died in his bed, at Torre di Sopra, and it seems that he yelled at the old cook who had looked after him for years. "Stop! I can't stand this pain, let me die!" Such was the spasm of his heart broken in two. It's strange that the heart he tried for years to preserve in a state of conservative paralysis, broke before any other organ, with the roar of a bomb exploding.

I remember his body on view in his sculpture studio with the large luminous windows. He was laid on a table draped in yellow. The doctor asked me to leave because he wanted to "give him an injection."

"And injection, if he's dead?" I insisted curious.

And he patiently explained that grandfather had left written in his will that he wanted an injection of poison in his femoral vein to be certain that he would not wake up after death in a coffin, because this terrorized him more than anything in the world.

I remember stories told in the evening after dinner in the always perfumed loggia under the Art Nouveau of my grandmother Yoi: they were stories of people who were presumed dead, who then awakened after being buried and knocked in vain against the roof of their coffin. Later, someone would open that coffin, but it was too late: the dead was found with teeth marks on their hands. To evade this, Grandfather had himself injected with the strongest poison. I instead have already indicated in my will that I want to be cremated. I have, in common with my Grandfather Antonio, an incurable repugnance towards everything closed. I don't choose to go inside caves. Never would I have been able to be a spelunker or a miner. Do women miners even exist? Or do those faces we find printed in newspapers, blackened by coal, rickety helmets on the head, elastic band tightening under the throat, eyes shining in the dark, belong only to male miners? A brief caption says that they died asphyxiated.

Papà gave her a Japanese doll.
    In this photo D. does not look pretty, but neither does the doll! writes my mother with unusual irony.

My young ethnologist father wanted me to become familiar with the myths and dreams of a culture different from ours. He didn't know that the initiation had already happened through the words of my ineffable and fiery nanny Miriokosan, who to make me fall asleep told me terrifying tales of cruel ghosts and horrifying inhabitants of foreign forests. Japanese children's stories are even more vicious than ours. And there is no need to disturb Bettelheim to imagine that their function is to reveal the little monster inside each of us.

The fairy tale my father told me, and I can see even now the gesture of removing the scarf from the face, is called *The Man Without a Face*. It's the story of a shepherd who roams with his sheep. One day, actually one evening, when the shadows are elongated, he sees a well-dressed man, wearing a hat, approaching from the woods. He thinks it must be a traveller who has lost his way and so waits for him, well disposed to have a chat; it's been days since he's seen another human being. When the man is within speaking distance, however, the shepherd sees that something is not right. The man's face is empty, without nose or eyes. He is horribly devoid of any recognizable traits, and walks with treacherous confidence into the void, suspended between earth and sky.

The shepherd understands that this is a ghost, and he begins to run towards the road, terrified. Every now and then he turns to see if the man without a face is following. And in fact, he sees him approach rapidly, as if he wants to tell him something. But what, if he doesn't even have a mouth? The shepherd crashes through the woods, arrives on the road and sees a truck headed towards town. He chases it as fast as he can, and when he reaches it, signals the driver, who brakes just in time for the young man to jump on so he can continue. The shepherd, breathless, sits down beside the driver and begins to tell him his story. "A ... a ... a maaaaan," he says, babbling, "a ... a man without a face." And the driver turns to him and, moving the scarf away from his face, says, "Like me?"

Even today I experience the chill that rose up the roots of my hair when my father would make this final gesture of revealing himself to the shepherd, who believed himself to be safe. My beloved father was a great storyteller when he felt like it; he had a great sense of suspense.

How many stories of ghosts, of vampires, follow the same pattern: the young protagonist has gotten away from a group of vampires who wanted to bite him and now he believes to be safe in the trustworthy arms of a mother or a wife, but on looking at her better, he becomes aware that in her tender smile there is a beacon of greed and between her lips involuntarily emerge two little sparkling fangs!

Papà or Mamà help D. onto skis, she complains as if to excuse herself, saying "Papà I don't know how to yet, I have to learn."

In fact she is too small. She only manages to make a few steps on flat ground. We don't insist. She loves instead to be pulled along on the sled. It's much more comfortable!

[...]

Every day I take her for a walk from 11 until 12:30.

15 or 20 degrees below zero.

Papa insists on wanting to teach her to ski, but D. is not so convinced that it's possible. She says, "I don't know how, Papà. I slide. I'm too small."

And then now and then when he's not here she says, "Mamà, now I am big, right? I want to put on my skis."

This thing about the skis has always been an ordeal. My father never let me have lessons. He put skis on my feet and said, "Go!" I learned like this, to approximately stay upright and to go straight. Only more than 30 years later did I take the initiative to pay an instructor, and to learn how to zigzag down, managing some rapid turns without falling.

Now, after having broken my femur when I was hit by a car while on my bike, I can no longer allow myself to fall, so I only cross-country ski. I don't want to give up the smell of snow. Some people would say that snow doesn't have a smell, but they would be wrong because the movement of the skis on that soft powder, the friction made by the wood that sinks in that frozen dust, provokes small waves of fragrance that discreetly touch the nostrils. And what about the light and graceful sound of cracked crust emitted by trampled snow?

Today, if I raise my eyes from my computer screen to look outside the window of my house in Pescasseroli, I see the small crystalline flakes fall on the green beech trees, and I feel sated in the quiet joy of existence.

She always wants to eat the snow and Papà gets angry, continues my mother.

And snow does not have a great taste, it tastes of water without salt, bland and cold. But it's the granular consistency that is attractive: like holding a snow-cone and nibbling it. In those moments, when warmed by a subtle sun I taste the cold granules, I wonder why I think of the title of a book, *Eating God* by Jan Kott. A title that has the power to fascinate every guest that comes to my house. If their eyes see that book, their hands reach to grasp it, to read eagerly. But can God be eaten?

I'm beginning to speak a little English with D. who is learning it …
I bought her her first book of Nursery Rhymes and I read it to her trans-
lating it.

She quickly learns "Jack Horner" sat in a corner, eating his Christmas
pie, he put in his thumb, and pulled out a plum, and said what a good
boy am I! And she repeats "Vat a gublemai!" then "Diccori diccori dock"
and some words from that. She begins to understand, "shut the door,"
"some water please," "come here," etc. If we spoke only English she would
learn it immediately.

But I didn't want to speak English, rather Japanese, that was the
language of the shopkeepers, of the children in the streets, of the
bus drivers, of the nannies and the teachers. I didn't care about Italy
which seemed to be a distant incomprehensible country. I wanted
to be like everybody else, in all respects a Japanese. That's why I
would happily put on a kimono, and I even learned how to sit for
hours with my legs folded, something I cannot do today. I tried to
speak dialect, and to invent word games with the wild children who
ran in the streets of Sapporo.

D. occupies all my time because she won't leave me for a minute (she
even followed me to the bathroom!) And she will not go to sleep unless
she is with me. At times, I am disheartened with this, but I hope that
I can change her habits. Now she is still anxious because of that endless
journey.

This physical dependency softens me. It makes me think of those
images we see on the screen when we listen to stories about monkeys that run through the branches of African forests: the nimble
mother who clings to the branches with her tail straight, carrying
on her back a little monkey with new, fluffy fur. There is a physical-
ity in the mother-daughter relationship that nothing in the world
can modify, and that binds the two bodies, the smaller one to the
larger one, in a natural embrace, even when they are far apart and

don't see each other, and symbolically recreates the first warmth of a dark primordial home.

The body that presents itself to the confused imagination of a child when it's born is that of the mother. A mysterious mountain that dominates and calms it, feeds it and also inspires fear. The thrill of that milk that flows down the throat, through the warmth of a nipple that is both pillow and cup … how to substitute it?

She loves to play with the snow and wants "to help Papà shovel the snow." I played at being big, but I was mindful of my sojourn in the protective waters of my mother. Every now and then, even now, I have a recurring dream when I am tired or upset. I find myself immersed in a lake at night. The water is light and lukewarm. And I feel calm. A line of orange lights crowns the lake, and makes me feel safe, in that I could reach the coast whenever I want. But I don't swim. I remain immersed in those warm waters that fulfill me. I rest my eyes on those reassuring lights reflected in the dark waters of the lake. And I think that I will end up swimming to arrive at the shore. But meanwhile, I am fine as I am: I enjoy my calm bath, silent, inside the earth's warm womb.

It's a delightful dream of peace. From which I exit re-invigorated. For many years I've asked myself what does it mean. Until I finally told myself that it certainly concerns an unconscious, poignant nostalgia for the womb. A little late at sixty, but imagination follows its own paths, not always recognizable with the logic of chronology.

D. is in school! The first few days I took her because she was a little afraid of the "nuns with the hats," but after that, she's enjoying it more and more, and she learns little fables and words in Japanese.

[…]

In the afternoon she naps. To fall asleep, she still wants her soother, (how embarrassing!) But I see no reason to forbid this little habit that might possibly stop her from getting others. In any case, a little at a time, I'll try to take it away.

[...] Every morning she takes her lunch (an egg salad sandwich, tomatoes and fruit). At school they give her a glass of milk. But at 2 when she returns, she is always hungry and Saka-san gives her whatever is available. I protest, but it's no use. So now and then, a light indigestion and milk of magnesia at night—it's miraculous. The following morning she awakens with a clean tongue and in a good mood.

Even then I suffered from "torcibudello", as my sister Yuki would say. "Twisting gut." "Do you have *torcibudello* this morning?" I have always had a weak stomach. Or perhaps I have what doctors call "irritable bowel syndrome" that I have constantly tried to ignore by eating everything. And I have almost accustomed my poor colon with its long loops, to see all types of food coming, hot, fat, foreign and spiced. Every now and then, however, it gets upset and rebels, it begins to tie itself into knots and produces the most agonizing pain. To calm the spasms of the nervous and impatient colon, I have to quickly lie in bed with a hot water bottle and breathe deeply. Then for a few days, I put myself on a diet of boiled rice and lukewarm lemon juice.

When the weather is fine, on Sundays, Papà, Mamà and D. go out together. The 14th of May—the Cherry Blossom Festival in Moroyama. First we go to see the people on the grass, under the trees, hundreds of them who eat, sleep. [...] D. is happy to look at everything—she buys sweets, a child's windmill—then we leave the crowd to go and eat on top of a small hill. Mamà is huge and a little tired. D. loves "sandwiches."

My mother was pregnant with Yuki. Even so, she came with us on drives and picnics. Swollen and a little tired but indomitable. She was always ready to pick me up if I couldn't keep up to the rhythms of my father's steps.

"Papà, when will we arrive?"

"In five minutes."

But those five minutes, I knew from experience, could become twenty and then twenty and then another twenty, entire days walking, waiting to arrive.

My sisters inherited from him the capacity to dilate time beyond measure. Not me. I am as punctual as a little soldier. And often, I am left standing there waiting. Margarethe von Trotta, with whom I've written two plays, used to say, "You're the Teuton, not me." And she'd say it while blowing in my face the pestilent smoke of a cigarette, knowing full well that I would have begun to sneeze and cough. She would smile cheerfully, seating herself on the windowsill of my studio. "Now I will promise you, I'll keep the cigarette out the window." Fortunately this was at the beginning of June. Actually, that flaunted smoke was her way of protesting against my drastic working hours, my demand that we begin work at nine in the morning and finish at eight at night.

My father always arrived late at the stations. "Papà, they've whistled. The train is about to leave." And he would begin to run, with my wrist held tightly in his fingers. At a certain point, I could no longer keep up with him. I would fall on my knees, but he did not stop. He continued, almost lifting me off the ground, dragging me. He would pull me up while the train was already travelling towards the next station.

At the first stop he would get up, restless. "I'm going to get something to drink."

"But Papà, what if the train leaves without you?"

"Don't worry. I'm going and I'll be back." And he would disappear. I would look out the window, my heart pounding, gripped by worry. I would see him alight with one leap and enter the station through large glass doors.

A few minutes would pass. The conductor would whistle. The train would begin to move, and I would feel the tears sliding down my cheeks. I had lost my father. How would I be able to find him when I didn't even know where we were to get off? But within five minutes, he'd pop up with a huge smile from the far end of the railcar, holding a bottle of fizzy water. "Here I am, Daciuzza. Where you scared?"

How true to ourselves we remain, though we alter so as to not rec-ognize ourselves. *D. loves "sandwiches and picnics,"* wrote my mother. Even today I love sandwiches and picnics. Often, with friends who always fill my house in the mountains, we make cheese and tomato sandwiches and we head out on the rocky paths of Mount Marsicano to stop under a maple or a hazelnut tree, beside a half-dry creek that emits a slight scent of rotten leaves, to eat our picnic.

I even like the preparation of a packed lunch: to cut the bread into slices, but neither too thick because it would be difficult to bite into them, nor too thin because they'd crumble. Then a thin layer of oil, a slice of cheese on top, then a barely visible slice of tomato, close it all with another slice of bread, and wrap the sandwich in a paper napkin. When you have a mound of these white bundles, you slip them into a large bag, then you cram it into a large backpack, with a thermos of cold tea, a handful of well-washed ripe plums, and carrots or cucumbers seasoned with salt and cut into strips. Someone else will bring one or two bottles of water, possibly not in plastic containers, though this is difficult, because glass weighs much more.

Then there's the slow, upward hike along rocky paths, the right fist curled around a stick picked up on the way. Then the explora-tion of the area and the search for the place to stop, which must be flat, even if on top of a steep rock, must have a little running water nearby to keep drinks cool, must be in the shade of a leafy tree, far from the excrement of cows carrying flies and horseflies, must be covered with clean grass, without too many thistles that prick and scratch. It is not easy to find such a place, especially in the wild Abruzzo mountains which are dotted with cows and sheep that graze freely, leaving their marks everywhere. And so, we have to walk a long way before stopping.

Fortunately, the cows and their excrement don't smell. They are herbivores. But they bring every species of insect. Sometimes if you look closely at a dry cow patty, you'll see that it resembles a beehive, sprinkled with holes and blocks in which hide the larvae and eggs of many species of insects. Those cows, with their crescent horns, white skin, and large, moist, black nose, with their slow dextrous movement among the trees and stones, make us think of a paradise lost.

They are the mildest and kindest creatures on earth. They ask for nothing, except to live. They eat grass, and despite their strength, are not capable of hurting a fly. They view the world with calm eyes just slightly surprised. I understand that in India, they are considered inhabited by a divine force, very pure, sacred to heaven and left to wander freely through the cities.

Even when they're sweaty and dirty they emit a pleasant smell of grass and hillsides. Yet on these mythical and heavenly animals, speculators have raged, trying to transform them from herbivores into carnivores, crippling their nature and causing them terrible diseases, which when discovered, they proceeded with the same brutality to exterminate them. Millions and millions of these creatures have been culled in general indifference. It is possible that animal pain is so little visible, so little communicable?

On Sundays and holidays now Papà and D. go out alone with Japanese friends. When D. gets tired, Papà carries her on his shoulders. At night, Dacina returns with red red cheeks and bright, shiny eyes.

My adorable mother doesn't explain that she didn't come with us because she was too far along in her pregnancy. And she would not have been able to move with ease along stones and rivers, scrambling through brambles.

Is that the moment in which the child in me fell in reckless love with my young, seductive father who was near me? I do not have a precise knowledge of the birth of this excruciating passion that filled my simple little life. And yes, instinctually, I felt closer to my mother. But while she was the rock to which I clung so as not to fall off the mountain, my father enraptured me with his absences and his fluctuating affection. He would travel to distant places alone, with his trusty heavy metal Leica, and would return laden with photographs of magnificent, inaccessible countries. Above all, the scents he brought back were foreign and difficult to decipher, scents of secret perfumed rooms, of light distant air, of earth with unknown grasses, of night skies of undiscovered stars.

D. grows, and almost every day she has a new expression. Often a serious serious little face, full of personality. She has a strong character—is stubborn and persistent—but gives in most of the time after a long period of reasoning.

It was an apprenticeship in logic, that is not always on our side. At what age do we learn that the rationalization of our interests is dangerous to our sense of truth? Reason was the aerial net that caught and stopped my flying dreams. In the long run, it always won against my stubbornness. Reason that excludes one's own interests, reason as an end in itself, reason that discovers the firm stones that halt the flow of our most daring challenges. Learning to use logic as a clear mathematical concept of thought was for me the hardest thing to grasp. Instinct always leads us to bend our minds in our favour: we like something, it makes us comfortable and therefore it is right. To rationalize one's self-interest: a widespread practice, especially among salesmen and therefore counter-educational. Deprived of any confidence in logic as an objective tool for understanding reality, and ready to shout to impose its truth against that of others, the politics of one's own interest end up trampled a thousand times under the shoes of the pure and disinterested joy of reason.

13 April 1939.
Photograph of Mamà.
D. plays with coloured paper and loves to scribble. Now she wants to draw people and is upset that she's not able to. But this is a good drawing! writes my mother brazenly, pasting a scrawl.

To a mother, even ugly ducklings are beautiful, they say in Naples.
   Despite the teachings of a fairy with sharp ears and a pointed nose, I never managed to harmoniously put colours to paper. The fairy was Adriana Pencherle, my art teacher in Florence at the school

of Santissima Annunziata, and the sister of Alberto Moravia. When she arrived, breathless, she truly seemed to have stepped out of a fairy tale of gnomes and enchanted forests, with her skirts swinging against her long legs, the folder under the arm, the curly hair that framed her long and pointed face, her expression always surprised. Among the many chubby, predictable teachers, among the many judicious and unimaginative heads, she stood out as a star of ingenuity and candor. Patience unravelled like a secret and quiet thread that slid from the clumsy pupils' hands to hers, which were long and delicate. She was inhabited by a timid, perceptive wisdom. She could laugh with her students and fill them with attention. Everyone was a little in love with the fairy Adriana. And she responded to these little enthusiasms with fleeting smiles of contentment.

10 July 1939
At 10:10 a.m. Luisa Yukiko is born
Weight 3.2 kg
Length 53 cm
Ugly—
Hair: dark blonde
Eyes: long thin dark (grey?)
Nose: enormous
Mouth: enormous
Colour of skin: macchiato
A small reddish mark under the right eyebrow
Papà and Mamà disillusioned because she was not male

The disillusionment of Mamà and Papà, but above all of Papà who wanted a boy, imprinted a shadow on her small child's life. Despite the love she was then filled with, it was as if that first disappointment made her feel like a little precarious guest in the house of life.

The next day Mamà is fine. Yuki ate well. D. has seen her and is excited. She wants to pick her up—wants to bring her candy, and wants to take her home!

We celebrate the birth of your little daughter! Yours, Masayosi Oeda and Hiroyuki Miyasawa.

Ribbons and bows of paper. Fingers are set in motion with an amazing skill and make up congratulatory knots. A little girl has come into the world. But where was she before? I knew she'd been in my mother's tummy. There she slept and drank like a fish. But before, before she took refuge in that carnal house, where was she? Was there a place where children rested, waiting to be born? Perhaps I asked myself these questions some years later, but certainly they have ancient roots. I remember the taste, that made me think of cold rice and zukemono, the sour, spicy pickled vegetables.

Questions about birth often went in pairs, like cherries, with those about death: was there a precise place where the dead went? And where was it? And from there, could they now and then appear on earth to say hello to those left behind or was it prohibited? Could they return to this world in another guise, as the Japanese believed, or were they forced to remain in heaven forever? And what was this heaven like? A garden with the scent of gardenia, where plants had branches laden with the sweetest fruit, and rivers of milk and chocolate? Or was it a blinding desert, where no trees grew and the poor dead wandered with tongue out because of the heat, and at night would slip into holes dug in the sand?

Even in photographs, my sister Yuki seldom smiles. Is it possible that in her eyes pain grew like a silent permeating shrub? Can parents' disillusionment create such pain in an unconscious girl who has just emerged from the darkness of a loving, friendly belly? It's difficult to say. The fact is that Yuki has always suffered from a subtle and incomprehensive self-hatred. She has had every illness. She hurt herself various times in dramatic ways. She was diagnosed with an ambiguous, mysterious disease[3] that little by little has crippled

---

3   Rheumatoid arthritis.

her fingers, silenced her voice—she had a beautiful singing voice, fluid and sweet, perhaps inherited from Grandmother Sonia—and that has prematurely led her to death. She went on tiptoe, so as not to disturb anyone, flattened by the weight of her secret discontent, encased in a pain calcified inside her bones. Her disappearance is a wound that can never heal. I try to hold her in my thoughts, like a friendly ghost, but she flees, escapes; where are you running to? Where? The dead tend to run away from us. They always become younger while we always become older. Little by little, we transform ourselves into their mothers and then into their grandmothers. But why don't they ever turn around?

And yet, in my memories I cherish some happy, carefree moments with my sister Yuki, who was a cross between ant and cicada, though certainly more the latter, always singing, joyful, on a branch, without thinking that winter would come and the branch would fall and she would find herself without food.

Nonetheless, in our cottage in Kyoto, when we ate the hot homochi, the small rice paste cakes dipped in cold soy, she seemed happy. And when in the dark in our beds, we repeated the terrifying story of the faceless ghost that my father loved, she appeared radiant and happy. And when we played Empire at the Santissima Annunziata school in Florence, running from one part of the courtyard to the other, bound in our gray pleated uniforms, she seemed content to be in the world. And when we walked from Bagheria to Aspra, bathing suits and sandwiches in our ruck sacks, and we'd see who could dive from the highest rocks of Mount Zafferano, she seemed to be in total harmony with her own body, without a doubt or a care in the world. And when I waited for her before school in the mornings in Rome, and she was always late, and often wearing two different coloured socks, when we laughed until our stomachs ached, there were no traces of fear in her calm eyes. And when, as adults, both married, we decided to prepare a Japanese meal, going together to buy fish at the market, and when we rolled rice and a little wasabi in dark seaweed, and poured hot water over green tea, there was a wise, elegant precision in her movements that predicted a long happy life.

But no. In that delicate fair body, my sister Yuki harboured a malaise that would eventually destroy her. The intensity of her pain I find in a photograph of when she was seven and we are about to go to school. Our mother had taken us to a traditional photographer from Florence, who with a flourish signed portraits that were in soft focus as per the cinematic fashion. In the photo, my head is bent, and I have a slightly lost but confident smile, maybe even a little selfish. Instead, she has hopelessly sad eyes, as if sensing a harsh and thorny future. In that childish, anguished look, the most atrocious thing is her surrender: a total and very sweet surrender to a disharmonious future.

This old Ainu made us the honour of "baptizing" Luisa Yuki according to the Ainu rite, my mother writes, who participated with some perplexity in her husband's grand maneuvers of multi-ethnic education, as it pertained to their daughters.

Yuki so tiny, white, clean, soft between those hairy, filthy arms ... but what a kind, good man! And everyone else wanted to hold her and take turns giving her a "welcome in her entrance in life."

The Ainu, who were the object of my father's studies for years in Sapporo are different morphologically from the Japanese, because they are tall and white skinned, with wavy hair. It seems they came down from the north eons ago, and survived in those frozen areas by hunting bears. After a thousand years of difficult survival with the Nipponese, they are now reduced to a few hundred old people, who no longer speak their language, and walk happy and content like manikins, under the glare of cameras and the attention of anthropologists, towards extinction.

My father arrived in time, in the 1940s, to meet some of these old hunters; he photographed them in their huts, during the rituals around the bear hunt, wearing their clothes with geometric black-and-white designs, their faces painted with pitch and carmine. Since then the situation has deteriorated to the point that they have now become historical citations.

Only once in Africa, with Pasolini and Moravia, did I feel a similar sensation faced by some naked Pigmies who seemed to be bidding a tormented goodbye to their traditions, to their earth. They were forest creatures, and the forests were—actually are—regressing, and the small Pigmies with their bright, very intelligent eyes no longer travel great distances to hunt. Even the animals have disappeared, having been either killed or distanced by the arrival of new plantations, new roads, new intensive farming. This is how nowadays the Pigmies are enslaved by the neighbouring people, or end up clowning for tourists and beggars.

The visitors filmed them, the lights of the television cameras made them sweat but they smiled affably, even a little narcissistically, because those exhibitions had now become an important source of income. Their skimpy thongs, their pathetic tufts of leaves are now only a theatrical accessory. They've lost everything: their language, their ancient knowledge, the science of constructing houses, of hunting, of speaking with animals. And they are reduced to the happy begging of a window display, and try to obtain the obtainable, with moral degradation in their hearts.

A stick-figure drawn by D. all by herself. Beneath it: *portrait of Yuki chan because "chichiai, chichiai."*

The attention towards my drawings seems to me frankly excessive. They were terrible drawings, that showed an absolute lack of talent in any form of graphic or pictorial art.

This does not impede me from being a frequent visitor of museums and art galleries. What moves me most in paintings is the mystery of a barely implied story. The intense secret paintings of

Rembrandt, the theatrical representations of Vermeer, the philosophical spaces of De Chirico, the silences of Pietro della Francesca, the ritual cries of Chagall.

"How many pairs of shoes have I worn out" going to museums when travelling! They are my most favourite destinations. Often, I stop there to eat. I like that art school air, the museum restaurants, where the wait staff walk on light shoes and seem to have jumped out of a Manet painting, the display cases laden with cakes that suggest the still life of a Flemish painter, and the air saturated by bluish hue.

I rush to the large monographic exhibitions, even if there is a queue for an hour, as happened to me in Paris recently with the large exhibition of de La Tour, that enamoured me forever. I had never seen so many paintings of de La Tour in one place. I had never fully appreciated the intense depth of the theatrical essence of this Lorraine artist. All the paintings are internal and gradually turn into palpitating stages of the mind. Exactly as happens on stages, the light comes from precise, recognizable and artfully arranged sources for dramatic effect. Shadows lengthen with chromatic intelligence on the mouths, hair, fingers, feet and reciting figures. The theatre must be one of the most mysterious rooms frequented by my mind. De La Tour has opened the doors of that room and has entered arrogantly, sat on a straw chair borrowed from a painting by Van Gogh, crossed his leg and started to speak, in a brooding voice of the France of his era, "Those tears, those tears of San Pietro, I don't know how he was able to trace them ... Even if my king, my Louis XIII, before he died told me: you do it, do it, but don't forget the tears of San Pietro ... It was a commission without conditions, but excessive freedom can also kill ... As much as I went back and forth with the brush, those tears didn't come to me ... poor Pietro, so alone in his repentance."4 The year was 1645.

A bottomless joy when the paintings come to life and tell stories.

---

4   St. Peter Repentant by Georges de La Tour, 1645 in Cleveland Museum of Art.

10 September—at exactly two months Yukiko began to look at her hands, and when we speak to her, she responds with little gurgles "grh"—"a-wru" etc.

Yukiko's umbilical cord is not right—we took her to the hospital to see Dr. Nagai and Tanagni—nothing serious—a small "granulation." We have to give her various medicines for a week.
    After seven days, all is well.

16 September twice a day she takes Patrogen (8 rounded "special" teaspoons at a time) the rest I give her at 4:30 a.m., 8-8:30 a.m., 12-1p.m., 4-5, 9-10 p.m.
    I'm not so worried about the exact time—depends when she awakens and whether she cries or not.

What can I say of this young scrupulous wife, who gets up at 4:30 in the morning to administer medicine to her sick daughter? Most likely everything would be better understood by knowing in depth the story of her childhood relationship with her mother, a beautiful woman, sensual and free enough to abandon her daughter to the care of her husband, who in turn became a patient and tender maternal father.

This is how the two sisters Topazia and Orietta loved their father, like an affectionate and patient mother-figure. While they harbored resentment over the careless abandonment of a mother too in love with herself. At a certain point, she even left home for another man. Her husband, outside of any Sicilian tradition, left her alone. And when she decided to return, he opened the doors to the house, with an indulgence that the daughters judged to be "excessive."

This being on the side of their father-mother, I believe, indissolubly united the two sisters: Top and Ori they called each other. Two girls so different that they seemed like night and day. Orietta dark, with black eyes, a luminous smile, timid and sullen. Topazia blonde with blue eyes, extroverted and sporty. They never parted.

They were affectionate, supportive, and even today, both in their 80s, they phone each other daily and hold each other's hands, even if they live in distant cities and have children and grandchildren that absorb all their energies. Orietta married a young Pisan, Gianni Guaita, tall, thin, taciturn, who has written a number of fine novels, highly intelligent apologues in theatrical form, and has had a passion for politics. In the 50s, he was a brave trade unionist, who participated with courage and self-sacrifice in the great peasant struggles for land in Sicily; he fought, risking his life against the mafia, often saving himself from the slaughterhouse, both by his enormous ingenuity that the mafia itself considered with amazement, and for his risky strategy of always telling the truth that in those lands at that time, transformed him into an alien.

I heard him now and then speak of his relationship with the "Duchess Sonia" who did not want to give him his beloved Orietta in marriage. Grandfather Enrico, who was indulgent, had said, "Go ahead do it, as long as Orietta is happy." But her mother, no, she wanted a different husband for her second born. She wanted an aristocrat or at least a wealthy man. Gianni was neither wealthy nor an aristocrat. And she made it tough for him, before giving him permission. Permission that, moreover, the two pigeons (that's what they called each other),had already taken, by living together. But in those times it was inconceivable to marry without the permission of both parents of the bride.

I was inspired by my mother's stories about life at Villa Valguarnera when she was a child, a place crawling with boys (first and second cousins) and I used this inspiration in my description of the life of Marianna Ucria and her brothers two centuries earlier. When I lived there, right after the war, already the huge beautiful villa was in a state of ruin: the walls were crumbling, the roof leaked, the statues in the garden had been stolen or chopped into pieces, and weeds invaded the splendid deck-garden. Furthermore, I didn't have cousins with whom to play. Orietta's children—the sweetest Anna, the one I'm most fond of, now lives in New York with her musicologist journalist husband Enrico, who teaches at the University of Florence; and Carlo who sculpts—all lived else-where, and I tumbled with the cowherd's daughters, Ena and Ina.

Yuki-chan and Mamà in a Yadoya in Tokyo. End of October '39. Yuki suckles slowly and is never sated before 25 min … Her stomach is not well. If I give her less milk, she cries desperately. The doctor sent me med-icine for Yuki-chan—7 August she is fine again.

How she curves over little Yuki-chan my beautiful mother in the photo my father took! This was something to become jealous of, after so many attentions all addressed to the eldest daughter. But instead, no, fortunately: *D. is loving with Yuki—she rocks her, she talks to her—she bottle-feeds her.*

The first years most influence a life. Could it be that because of this childish propensity for motherhood, I have never suffered from envy and jealousy? Could it be that the good relationship estab-lished with my little sister has permitted me to escape the clutches of the fear of abandonment? Could it also be the explosive generos-ity of my mother did not belong in that negative place?

However, it's also true that right at the birth of my sister, I got an ear infection. If I wanted to refer to *The Book of the Id: Psychoanalytic Letters to a Friend* by Groddeck, for an interpretation, I could say that I have deflected my natural jealousy by aiming the aggressive-ness toward myself. Could this be it? The exclusivity of children has the shape of an iceberg buried under the waters of undefined emotions. One cannot see its size, but it is capable of sinking a ship, if its underground mass meets the ship's hull.

December 10, Tokyo.
D. had an operation done by Dr. Stedefelt at the General Hospital in Yokohama. We went to the hospital—beautiful—super clean—ele-gant—run by British, Russian, French and Japanese nuns. At 12 o'clock the first injection—nothing. At 1 they took her away. Neither Fosco nor I were allowed in the operating room. At 2:20 she returned on a stretcher—unconscious, vomiting black bile, with the danger of

*suffocation because she was unconscious. **I really thought she was going to die. Breathing through instrument—horrible to see and hear. After 2 hours woken—"Mamà" quarrelled with the** director **who won't let me stay by her "she doesn't understand, she is absolutely unconscious [...]."** I went and she embraced me crying "Mamà, Mamà doshite meme ma gate no" so pathetic staring round*[5] *with her pupils dilated by the ether.*

It has remained a habit of my mother, this, to speak in English in difficult moments. Interweaving it with Italian and Japanese. I think it comes from her British teachers about whom she often spoke.

"**I am an agnostic,**" Miss Ingram would say.

And my mother asked, "What does agnostic mean, Papà?"

"It means that she abstains from all religions," her father said. "But you, Topazietta, still have to learn all about various religions, then you can decide."

"'I am agnostic,' Miss Ingram repeated monotonously, putting her hands behind her head," my mother tells me, smiling.

Grandfather Enrico was a modern, enlightened man. He could smile at the rigidity of others; he was indulgent with his wife's whims; he tried to guide his daughters without being noticed. He was a vegetarian and a follower of Steiner, whose vegetarian cookbook still circles the world.

"Miss Ingram was spartan and frugal. She made us go out no matter what the weather, be it rain, mud, snow. She was scandalized when the Sicilians said, 'Poor little children, with this cold ...' For her, the body had to be governed by the sound of a whip: no laziness, languor, whining, procrastination. You had to do your duty, always and completely.

"She had fixations: for example women's heels in patent leather. She could not bear them. For us young women, she ordered men's shoes, low and casual. She was all about health: porridge with milk in the morning, at noon she allowed us to sit at table with our families,

_____

5 Bold text here is in English in the original.

but we were not to open our mouths. Never speak to adults if not spoken to. In the evening, she let us have a cup of hot chocolate and two slices of bread and butter. Then to bed. Then in the morning I had to have a bowel movement at eleven. She would lock me in the bathroom and I until I'd had it, I couldn't leave. I still do this today."

Aristocratic Sicilian families were accustomed to bringing a governess for their children from abroad, but mostly from England. There is no need to be familiar with the Brontë sisters' novels to imagine the life of these young women, who tiptoed into the wealthy mansions of the Sicilian aristocracy, stoically facing the immense differences in mentality, tastes, habits. They would stay away from home for years, segregated in dormers, devoted to solitude, usually treated with kindness, but never truly admitted into family life. Paid little, the governesses lived a dignified life, and with strict rules raised the stunned girls to whom they had become attached.

But just when they had learned to coexist with the complicated characters of the Islanders and their "barbaric" ideas, when they had succeeded in seeding the root of affection in the hearts of their pupils, they had to abandon them to their destiny of wives, and to depart for another house, another family, with little baggage, and much bitterness in their thoughts.

The revenge, when possible, consisted in conquering the male heart of a father, a brother to take as far as the altar, as the talented Brazilian director Maria Luisa tells us in her moving film *Miss Mary*. But this happened very rarely.

"I had three governesses," my mother tells me today, with her unmistakeable cool Argentine voice, while sitting on my Roman balcony: "Miss Ingram the Scottish, Miss Healey and Miss Toovey. Miss Healey was a Victorian by education and spirit, proud to have been presented at Court, to have frequented governess school. She was an excellent social educator: she taught us how to show reverence for old aunts, the elderly, married people, how to pronounce sentences in English, how to be kind to everyone, especially to subordinates. We had to kiss the hand of Mamà and Papà, and I did it until I was 16. She taught us how to hold our forks at the table, how to clean one's mouth before drinking, how a girl should never speak and can answer only if spoken to, but cannot speak in the presence of adults until she gets married.

"Miss Healey the formalist: not mean but classic. She walked around the house wearing gloves, and a hat on her head. When Prince Umberto of Savoy came to Palermo, I was invited to the dinner of honour, but not before taking an exam, which I passed, thanks to the teachings of Miss Healey. She was already old when she came to us, and when leaving our family she decided to stay in Palermo, where she died years later, in a small, dignified apartment, all alone. Papà gave her a living, knowing that she had nothing: in those days, there were no pensions, no insurance, no long exits. She was poor, but very proud of her nephew, director of the Port of London.

"Miss Toovey was much younger and more modern. She studied archeology and had come to Palermo for this, then finding herself without money, had decided to be a governess. It was she who one day let me go out alone, something unheard of in those times. I remember that she consulted Papà, who made me give my word (lies were and are a crime in England) that I would not stop for any reason, that I would go along Via Libertà, without going into the patisserie, without stopping with anyone, and that I would have returned home, always proud and silent. After I was out ten minutes, came the alarmed phone call from Aunt Felicita. 'What are you doing? Are you crazy? You're letting your daughter go out alone in the streets?' And Papà said, 'I gave her my permission.' One by one, Zia Felicita had to reassure all the family, who were upset by my going out.

"Miss Toovey was a very cultured woman, she was well versed in modern literature and with ancient ones too. She was a great reader of Shakespeare, whose verses she made me learn by heart, and for this I thank her because they still keep me company. I finished my high school with her. Except that instead of a Baccalaureate, I wrote the entrance exam for the Academy of Fine Arts ... She made me study Chaucer, Thackeray, Dickens. She also loved geography, she knew the rivers and mountains of all the world. She wore her hair in a pixie cut, a *la garçonne*, something that was considered very daring back then. She was intelligent and free. She, Orietta and I would go out in three, and she would explain to us the beauty of landscape, of architecture.

"One Sunday when there was no one to leave me with, and she wanted to go to the Anglican church, she asked me if I wanted to go with her. I was undecided, and didn't know what to do. I knew that Aunt Felicita would disapprove. Then Miss Toovey took me by the hand and took me to 'your father the duke' as she called him. She asked him if she could take me to the Anglican church, something that sounded very provocative in a city of formalistic Catholics. Papà looked at me affectionately and said, 'Go ahead, but don't let yourself be influenced by one credo over another. There are many religions and you are not old enough to decide. And don't be arrogant enough to keep yourself above religion. Faith is an important, beautiful thing. But you have to practice it with conviction. Go ahead, and trust Miss Toovey, who is an objective person.'

"Aunt Felicita, who was the older sister and watched over the eight younger brothers—her mother had died during the childbirth of her ninth—was scandalized by this open-mindedness of Papà, but then adjusted because she was mild-mannered. Aunt Felicita was also very fond of her niece Maria, who was the most beautiful of the Alliata sisters, and had married a Di Napoli, with whom she had six children, four of whom died of tuberculosis."

In short, several knowledgeable and austere British women determined the first customs of my mother's life. Customs that even when contradicted, reversed, put underfoot, tend to somehow resurface.

It would be interesting to study Sicilian history in relation to the young women teachers, whether British or German. There were many families who hosted rigid Northern teachers and generations of Sicilian girls grew up adopting the myths and precepts of an adventurous and resolute England.

Imagine a poor Victorian Scottish girl plunged into the baroque villa of an aristocratic family in Palermo at the beginning of the century. Grandfather Enrico, philosopher, passionate about oenology, kind and rational. Grandmother Sonia all irrationalism and passion, certainly adorable as a young woman, but insufferable with age. How to reconcile a severe Britain with a soft Sicily, as they seemed to be in the popular imagination? Probably in the only way possible, or by applying without leniency, without asking yourself too many questions, the rules and disciplines of your country trying not to dwell on the habits of a mysterious and complicated, dramatic and contradictory island.

Grandmother Sonia did not seem too interested in what passed through the minds of the British teachers of her two daughters. It was more Grandfather Enrico who, with his phlegm and his philosophical curiosity, observed the poor involuntary exiles and was overtaken with pity and tenderness. Grandmother Sonia, who could easily speak English, French and German, who could read music, and had a cultured knowledge of opera, lacked those fundamental readings that had been instrumental in the formation of her husband.

Voltaire, Montesquieu, Rousseau were all unknown to her. She had never intellectually stepped out of the garden of her house. Imagine the forests and deserts of a distant and unknown continent! All her energy and talent that certainly would have made a great impression on a stage, were highjacked by small amorous schemes. As if every conquest compensated for the splendid career of opera singer she had given up. She was stingy and grandiose at the same time; she had developed since the birth of her daughters, a rivalry that made her uncertain and authoritarian. In other words, an unhappy woman who tended to "make others" pay, whether they were daughters or husband or friends. While capable in certain occasions of being very gentle, generous, and affectionate, she soon tired of "being good" and would let herself be captured by her anxieties, that joined music with Eros.

My mother has certainly suffered much from these shortcomings which, like all daughters eager for attention, she has interpreted as personal injuries. Her heart has never forgiven the beautiful Sonia for having neglected her. And perhaps, just to compensate for this void, she has been so generous, so excessive in arching over my little life with the fervour of a neophyte.

Under Yuki's photo: "Momo Taro San." Momo Taro was a baby born from a peach. An elderly couple, grieved at being barren, asked the gods for grace. The next day, while the farmer was hoeing the earth, a peach fell from the bush full of fruit. He picked it up, opened it and found inside Momo Taro, a plump, strong child … my little sister with her melancholy eyes. Born in July, daughter of the sun, but a sun perhaps too intense for the gaze of a delicate and generous child. However, the casing of the fruit that fell from the tree was good for her. Her girlish skin was pink and smooth like that of a Japanese peach.

She and I were united and bonded for four years. Then we became three, with Toni, born during the war, under the sign of Scorpio, like me. I can clearly recall her voice when, at Yuki's death, she said, "We are left in two." That trinity had been a fertile field for us girls, then young women and then adults with our own children. That fragile and strong trinity made us project great things for a shared future—childish resolutions like building a home theatre under the sea. There, we would dine at round tables with blue linen tablecloths, and dedicate ourselves to our favourite activities. Raising our eyes to the immense windows, we would be able to watch cod, squid, puffer and catfish swim by in floating seaweed. Those fish were not for be eaten, but only to be admired for their evolution and their quiet and determined passage. I would be in charge of the kitchen, because even then I was exhibiting talent for cooking, Yuki would cheer up everyone with her guitar and her voice, and Toni would dance.

Never has a childish project been dreamed in such detail by three sisters, who then proceeded to travel three different roads.

Only Yuko kept her promise: she dedicated herself to music and singing. She gathered popular songs from around the world, and specialized in ethnic music: she learned to accompany herself on the guitar. When her daughter Yoi was old enough, they began to play flute and guitar together. Or they sang together. It was a joy to hear them: they were excellent in counterpoint, they alternated playing the flute, indulged in daring duets, and created rhythm by tapping their feet on the ground.

At another time, we longed for large flights aboard a hot air balloon, where we would sing and eat and sleep, going up and down according to the winds, moving to the tops of the mountains, falling to touch the skin of the sea. We would have brought with us a goat and some frogs. Nothing else. Adults were not allowed, nor mice, in that flying house for three sisters.

All these dreams fragmented when the eldest—that's me—fell in love with a dark, laughing boy who knew how to tell the silliest jokes gracefully. At that point, I distanced myself from my sisters, searching more solitary avenues. In the meantime, however, a catastrophe occurred: Mamà and Papà decided to separate ... And as much as I have always theorized the rationality of divorce, I believe it was a complete loss of our sense of unity, even among sisters. An earthquake that flung us out of the security of affections, out of a single house, out of a common city, out of the same country. Toni, in fact, went to America to study, and afterwards lived in Morocco where she met her husband and had two daughters. I emigrated to Rome with my father, while Yuki remained in Sicily with Mamà. Then, as soon as she could, she married a blonde, gentle graphic artist and had a beautiful, difficult daughter who she named Yoi after our paternal grandmother.

Shouldn't sisters, joined by blood and by familiar habits, always remain together? I remember a photo shoot of the Le Kessler Twins, the famous variety dancers. So elegant and sober even when they were wearing skimpy stage costumes, and dancing in perfect harmony with the sound of Da da umpa, Da da umpa ... The two sisters had aged, had married and then separated and lived together, perhaps in two contiguous apartments, on the same landing, united for life. I've always wondered if it's only twins who share this fusioned fate or whether it can happen to brothers and sisters not born on the same day.

The image of the Kessler twins, so similar as to be confused, is superimposed on the vision of two other bodies united by twin ties: Matteo and Giovanni, two tall boys, very cultured, in love with music and mathematics. Matteo was my friend when I lived alone in Via Antonazzo Romano near Ponte Milvio. He would come to visit in the afternoons. He would sit in my wicker armchair and explain the laws of economics. He was serious, very serious and very shy. It was he, who made me understand the difference between the right and necessary direct taxes and the unjust and oppressive indirect ones. "... You can judge the degree of a country's democracy by the amount of direct taxes it can impose ... Of course it is much easier to act on indirect taxes, which do not take money only from those who have it, but from everyone indiscriminately. It is the system of weak governments destined to end up in the hands of the most powerful, who will do their best to harm the most fragile."

I think it was his shyness that kept him from telling me he loved me. But his eyes spoke for him. However, I too, was timid and would not have been the first to initiate words of love. I knew he had a twin brother, but I'd never seen him. Then I heard that this twin brother was gravely ill. Matteo began to come less and less. He was nervous, he would get up constantly, as if he were seated on thorns, but he never discussed his worries with me. A while after this, I left for Brazil and when I returned, someone told me he'd died. I couldn't believe it. I continued to see him standing by the window or seated with his hands, palms up, on his knees, his glasses that slipped down his nose, his cheeks always flaming. Only afterwards did I understand that his twin brother Giovanni, after much suffering and the total loss of use of his legs, had asked Matteo to give him a good death. Matteo had obeyed, but soon after had killed himself. In two, they didn't add up to fifty years.

3 May—Yuki chan first tooth.
6 May 1940 Yuki chan vaccinated—day 12 fever—day 13 less—day 14 pale and tired.

10 July 1940
Yuki chan 1 year old. […] For the first time dressed as a little girl in a skirt, but she doesn't like it because she can't easily crawl (her specialty) throughout the whole house ("guru-guru").
Yuki tried to sing! Hilarious. I've never heard a 10-month old baby try to do anything but talk. Now she says, "ittai" and "ba" and "Uchi-chan" as well as "tata, dada, bab, ciacia."
14/5 D. took the money I gave her to put in her purse and went alone to the market to buy a packet of candy (15c.!) How I would have loved to see it! First time that she knowingly uses money to buy something.

This was the education that made many mothers and grandmothers tremble: how could you let your little daughter go to the market all by herself? How could you give her money? How could you send her out on the street without accompanying her?

Oh yes, my very young and daring parents believed in a Montessori education, an education in responsibility. Very little appreciated both by the Palermitans with whom I found myself living after Japan, and by the teachers of the Florentine college where I was boarded for three years. Sicilian training was definitely an incentive to lies and fiction. Everything was possible as long as it was covered by the coils of an absolute and ruthless secrecy. The loss of virginity, adultery, trafficking under the table, the deception of the laws, everything could be remedied, as long as the image of decoration remained immutable and unchangeable. I still recall the mysterious aura of a friend in Bagheria who told me of a family secret during the war: "We didn't have anything to eat, but Mamma did not want our neighbours to know, so every day, she would put a little piece of lard on the stove, so that the smell would spread and so everyone thought that in our house we didn't need food." I, who came from an upbringing steeped in honesty, found it an absurd deception. But I did not imagine that those deceptions would have made me suffer much.

The sphinx's arcane smile alluded to a paradise familiar to everyone, though nobody knew its location. The consequences were the chasms that stretched between saying and doing. Chasms that were not considered dangerous or immoral, but only part of the daily burden: It was the banal and predictable, absolutely immutable texture of reality. The same that today says to a government minister: "The mafia has always existed, and we have to get used to it and co-exist with it."

Education in the Florentine school was based on sacrifice and privation. Despite being a lay boarding school, morality was calculated with grades and was rigorous: pink report cards for those who had behaved according to the rules, white report cards for those who had been between good and evil, gray report cards for those who had fallen into temptation. The confession of sins, however, saved one from damnation, and forgiveness from above consoled the most anxious hearts.

However, my enterprising affectionate mother talks about money. *It is the first time*, she says, that her eldest daughter spends her own money knowingly (money that her parents put in her purse so she would consider it hers).

I am reminded of a bus trip to visit Uncle Nicolino in Vallombrosa. I would have been thirteen years old. I still remember the enormous satisfaction, almost a physical pleasure in buying my own ticket, in waiting for the bus under a green canopy, with my suitcase beside me. I saw myself emerging from a movie. Ready to sing my joie de vivre. Does money give freedom? "Remember that for women, the word 'freedom' often means libertinism," says a

Dacia Maraini

friend of mine who teaches history at the university. And she looks at me with sad eyes.

Maybe in Vallombrosa I would have put on the silver swimsuit with the orange edges that I loved, and I would have performed a routine in the hotel pool. Like Esther Williams. Who knows if I would have been capable of coming out of the blue waters first with my legs, then my torso, and finally my arms and head, like her, always smiling and self-possessed. How was she able to so gracefully combine the professionalism of an acrobat and the smile of a young girl with a pure heart? Braided into her brown hair, Esther always had two tiny white roses. But didn't the roses flake off when she dove underwater for at least two minutes? "They are plastic roses, my child, totally fake, without life and without scent." But I didn't want to believe that. Esther, I was certain, picked a bouquet of fresh roses every morning from the garden of her villa near the sea, and with her long, tanned fingers wove them into a thread of raffia which she then knotted at the nape of her neck. Was this libertinism?

Our imagination was nourished by American films praising positive feelings. Deborah Kerr's great deeds, Rita Hayward's barefoot dancing, Doris Day's joyful singing, and Ingrid Bergman's languorous amorous promises. The villain, who would make you smile today, was always punished in those films. And the heroines opposed the heroes with seductive smiles, as if in a medieval contredanse: in front the girls with their light clothes, their slender waists encircled by a white belt, their breasts protruding under light and soft sweaters, their hair waved by a hot iron, their mouths painted in the shape of a heart. And now the girls to the back, and the boys in front: the sloppy Fred Astaire, the marauding Cary Grant, the languid Gregory Peck. And then, hop, join two-by-two, circle the room. That room lived in my eyes and whirled joyfully.

Money? Certainly we were short of it; certainly it would have been better to have had a little more. "But what would you be willing to do for money?" was the question from one of my school friends, who stared at me with serious, intelligent eyes. "Would you sleep

82

with a stranger for money? And how much would you ask?" my friend insisted, and it seemed above all, that she was asking herself, without finding a valid answer. In reflecting on it, I realized I would not be able to stand a stranger's hands on me, not even for a million dollars. Perhaps that's where the secret was, the difference between who does and who doesn't. Not to do with morality, but in the demand for a choice and awareness of one's own inalienable sexuality. I learned much later that many of the things said about the selling of oneself are arbitrary: the cliché is to consider the woman who gives sex in exchange for money a person of irrepressible, indomitable sensuality. It is no coincidence that the insult for girls who claim to make love when and with whom they want is a "whore." Instead, it's exactly the opposite: intense sensuality requires a freedom of choice that is not reconciled with any form of surrender to the desire of others. "I don't like the imposition of the contract already decided, the prepared bed and the mechanical gestures, even if in exchange for hard cash," I would tell my friend, who was very beautiful and who was probably trying to find justifications to resist the temptation to sell the only thing of which she was rich: her body.

"A married man, you know, is in love with me and wants to take me to a hotel ... He gave me a ring, but how could I justify this to my mother? I exchanged it for a purse and two cashmere coats ..." These were the confidences of a girl who was not secure in her sexual tastes and was attracted by the blaze of adult secrets. "He has a daughter my age ... she's beautiful, he showed me a photo ... He says he adores me ... he's so careful ... He's terrified at the thought of being seen with me." She was very proud of that clandestine love, flattering and promising.

Later on, I understood that this was a rather widespread practice among the girls at the school. Some seemed proud of their early earnings, an economic conquest obtained with the casual use of a body that cinema, television and lots of advertising suggested was made for this. An easy and degrading thing. Absolutely normal. Something two male hands, who have caressed you with delicacy and passion, can push you towards. Without regrets. Without questioning. It was so easy to get that money, and at the same time, so difficult. "You only have to think: that's not me, and all is well." "But if you look at your fingers covered in money, you feel yourself sinking in humiliation …" The most obvious thing is that the man who had held her in his arms, whispering sweet words, had suddenly become an enemy. He warned her not to speak to anyone. He sanctioned a contract with precise rules: you yield your young, virginal, forbidden body, and I will yield bank notes, one on top of the other, without saying a word. But everything ends there. She was still unaware of the sex market, and that figure seemed huge, while for him it was a small thing, given the enormity of the purchase.

Back to the money: my sweet mother has always had a propensity for debts—tomorrow a loan comes due, where to bang my head to find the money? We'll need to ask for another loan and then a larger loan to pay the first one, and then when that one comes due, a third gigantic loan. A treadmill that terrorized me. I saw how she spent sleepless nights, wondering about the deadlines of those blessed promissory notes that I imagined as fat and insatiable deities who fed on desperate mothers and hungry children.

I think it was a decisive lesson from which I learned that debts are as prolific as rabbits. If two debts have a child, surely within a month or two, there will be grandchildren and then grandchildren of the grandchildren and so on in a geometric multiplication system that will lead you directly into the mouth of a dragon ready to devour you in one bite.

In my life, I have avoided accruing even the smallest debt. If I had the money to pay, good, if not, too bad. I preferred to renounce a loved object rather than buy it on credit. And today, even $10 owed upsets me.

This debt avoidance forced me to find work immediately. I adapted myself to work as a secretary, a delivery girl, a file clerk, running up and down around the city delivering packages, jumping from bus to tram.

For many years, I lived, we lived, in poverty. Above all, in the postwar period in Sicily. Those were difficult years for everyone: there was no money for clothes, for butter, for meat, for medicine. I remember for a long time I wore a coat made from my grandfather's worsted wool cloak turned inside out several times. And my shoes were constantly being resoled, with patches all over.

At ten years old, I dreamed of owning a watch. Every day, I wrote to my mother from the boarding school in Florence asked her to send me a wrist watch. All my friends had them, and I didn't. In our family, we didn't have money for a wrist watch, something that was very expensive at that time. It was a luxury that not everyone could afford. But since I insisted and insisted, for Christmas my mother sent me an old small square alarm clock that had been transformed into a wristwatch with two new straps that I had to carefully close around my child's wrist. It was, however, too heavy and tended to slide onto my hand, revealing its alarm clock nature. It's obvious that I never wore it because I was too embarrassed, and I kept it under my pillow. I liked, however, its nocturnal clicking and the certainty with which it indicated the hours, festively illuminating the numbers on its square.

That grotesque clock leads me directly to a delightful story in *The Butterfly of Dinard* by Montale in which he narrates a tale about a bizarre travel alarm clock that he and his wife owned and had baptized "Angiolino" because it rang whenever it wanted to. They spoke of it as of an unpredictable baby son:

"The baby is in the suitcase. I laid it to sleep," says Mosca in the adaptation I did several years ago for radio.

To which Montale says: "It's immoral to call it a child ... Angiolino is only a clock."

And she says, "But you said it's like our son. He always travels with us. Don't you dare offend him."

But right at that moment, Angiolino begins to ring insistently. "Is it him?"

"It's him. But why does he have to ring at this hour?"

"Tonight, if you'll let me, I'll wind him up."

"If Angiolino begins to misbehave we're done."

"He's not misbehaving. It's you who wound him up wrongly."

"I wound him up perfectly."

"Are you saying that he moved the hands by himself?"

"It happens sometimes. The hand slides down, like a strap off a shoulder. Poor Angiolino."

And Montale concludes, "Enough with this childishness. No spurious children, no good things in bad taste, no gloomy feelings. We need to think about real things. Do you want us to try? Should we begin now?"

I too was torn between objects that speak and are treated a little like children, and concrete things that were proposed to my mind with the precise solidity of daily logic.

I cut D.'s hair, writes my mother, *she looks a lot older—[the haircut] accentuates the curve of her neck and her face.* This written under a photo in which I am kneeling like a Japanese girl on a tatami with a friend at Otaru in Toshiko's house. *D.'s kimono (a bit big!),* comments my mother, *red satin with bright yellow obi—gorgeous. The last photo with her long hair.*

Is it a coincidence that long hair here is combined with a position of mute yielding given to female composure?

Barring when I was at the school in Florence, I would never again have long hair. As if with that cut, my mother indicated a choice of quickness, of sobriety, of decision. A subtle yet unclear desire for emancipation? I don't know. But I was the one to decide that time. By losing my long hair I lost a certain childish tendency to seek protection, was pushed with affectionate hand out of the most archaic area of seduction. It is no coincidence that the whole history of religious fanaticism is linked to the regulation of women's hairstyles. Muslim fundamentalism resolved the issues by forcing women to completely hide their hair. But even the Catholic church, through the mouth of Saint Paul, have restrictive laws: "Man must not cover his head because he is made in the image and glory of God; the woman instead is the glory of man. In fact, man does not derive of woman, but woman of man. Because of this, the woman must wear the sign of her dependence on her head, because of the angels."6 Who knows why the angels were "the reason" for the covering of the head ... What seductive power lay in that tangle of dead cells as a dermatologist I know calls it? How many fears did it arouse in the burning hearts of our ancestors?

For Samson, the cutting of the hair was the beginning of the end. He lost, along with the "dead cells," all his physical energy and power. But for a blonde child who lived in a foreign country about to immerge itself in a massive world war, could it not represent an incentive to confirm her love of freedom? Was this my mother's secret wish? A strange symbolic destiny for hair: for a man to cut it means falling to the mercy of enemies, for a woman it means raising a flag of autonomy.

My mother knew about freedom. She had kept hers despite the injunctions of the nuns who in a Palermo boarding school claimed to let her bathe in the tub full of water, while wrapped in a floor-length nightgown ... Soap had to slide on the skin as if it were carried by a disembodied hand, by mechanical force, without looks of pleasure, both one's own and those of others. A woman's body was sinful even when she was very young and innocent. Perhaps even more dangerous because it aroused "evil thoughts" in males and could entice them to violent possession.

But the perfection of a Catholic education consisted of transforming woman into an accomplice to her mutilated fate. In silence, with joy, she ended up submitting to the fate that was set for her: she did it easily and also with enthusiasm (but moderately only, please), giving approval to her mental and physical castration.

---

6   According to a Hebrew saying, when the woman untied her hair and began to turn her head in a circle, the angels fell from the sky, because loose hair and dance were considered sexually libidinous, this saying is likely to refer to the episode of the fall of the angels of Gen. 6, 1-5.

What constraint is more effective than that which is implemented with the consent and the sanction of the interested party? She not only accepts her enslavement, but participates in the diffusion and maintenance of the ideology that consecrates and ideologizes it, considering it a natural part of her fate. This is what was done to women: it is the biggest crime. Rendered complacent in their servitude and transformed into obedient guardians of the rules that they then impose on their daughters and granddaughters.

When I think of the encounters in Africa, with Elmolo girls who had to be castrated (cutting of the large and small labia as well as the clitoris) I can only recall voiceless, hidden resistance. The girls said they tried to postpone marriage as much as possible, just to avoid being subjected to that terrible operation. But it was the mothers, the aunts, the grandmothers who insisted. And in the end, however rebellious they were, they had to give in. Then when they reached seventeen, eighteen, the family chose a husband for them, then isolated her in a hut just outside the village. There, an older woman, aided by two relatives, tied the legs of the promised bride to a tree trunk, and without anesthetic, with a knife disinfected in the fire, cut out all the sensitive parts of the female genitalia.

Once the vulva was reduced to a huge wound, the cut was stitched up with thin twine and therefore the future bride could rest for 15 days. After that time which served to soothe the most lacerating pains, began the wedding feast in which the whole village took part with masks, and songs and dances. Finally, after three days of drinking and eating (in this occasion several goats were sacrificed, and if the girl came from a wealthy family, also some cows) the bride and groom were left alone in their hut and the husband had to penetrate the young bride forcing himself into the aching wound. Grit your teeth and bear it, dear girl, you can do it very well, if you cry it means that you are not a woman but a senseless child. The whole village would laugh and blame her if she complained. So silence and abandonment, in the dark of night, to marital rape.

When she became pregnant, the whole community was delighted with the great wealth it would have enjoyed. And when she went into labour, the old surgical woman came to remove the stitches from the bride so that she could give birth to her son. After that, always the same old woman, carefully stitched up the cut so that every sexual encounter would forever more remain a torture.

The application of this cruel law is managed and controlled by the old women of the community. In the eyes of the village they appear as executors of a law desired by the gods and therefore fundamental. Amen. Meanwhile, the community has secured, even symbolically, absolute control over female sexuality.

A question rises at this point: but if women didn't give birth, could all this occur? If women did not get pregnant, would anyone care about their virginity or sexuality? Since the female body has the great gift of nourishing, growing, giving birth to an heir—the control of the future for every society, modern or ancient, passes through her womb. The castrations in some countries are physical and have ancient traditions, in others are symbolic.

Whether for bad or good luck, I can't say, female reproduction is not tied to sexual pleasure. A woman can become pregnant twenty times without having felt any pleasure. The man's penis, however, to emit his seed, needs desire, arousal, erotic ecstasy. This is why male pleasure has always been so celebrated and protected and also spoiled. To avoid hindrances, claims and for the safety of paternity, we pretend that female pleasure does not exist, or if it exists, it is placed in the list of abnormalities, deviations: a perversion for certain cultures, a dirty thing for others, a dangerous challenge to heaven for the warrior societies, who are accustomed to rigorously divide tasks between the sexes.

"It's this, you know, that historically has aggravated the condition of women," my historian friend tells me. A girl who has aged prematurely by making waves, and is called in a derogatory tone 'the feminist.' "They're considered important for reproduction, but to be kept under control, demonized when they show autonomy in pleasure, made complicit in their submission, with detailed teaching that instills in their hearts the idea of belonging to a lower, weaker, more unreliable, more dangerous, more restless, more sentimental race, and therefore in need of guidance, protection, precise directives. Here she is, Woman, dear Dacia, who gets angry, who denigrates herself, who throws herself away, who distresses herself, who feels guilty ... do you feel sorry for her? I can't hate her, however, you know, never, not even when she gets angry and sows traps for the unfortunate. The 'gold diggers,' for example, as the Americans call them, the young ladies of fortune, the femme fatales. Not even those can I condemn. It's the low self-esteem, the long practice of enmity towards other women that has made them like this, whether they're good or bad, they don't know it. They are absolutely blind and they have a great desire to live. They believe they are maneaters, and don't realize that they will always be eaten, because the male they think they dominate, considers them a little sordid, a little wicked, a little treacherous, a little deadbeat, a little dangerous, a little different, but all together so much, so much so, as to want to eliminate them."

My friend had a son, whom she educated according to her ideas, yet today he makes fun of her, steals her money, goes out in packs with his friends to undermine younger girls. "An absolute failure," she says, distressed. "I don't know how or when I lost him."

"Maybe he does it on purpose, out of spite," I venture timidly.

"I learned at my expense that community is stronger than family. My teachings have been overwhelmed by what he learned on the street, at school, with his classmates. It is there that he finds himself, it is there that he recognizes himself as a male. And yes, I love him so much, you know, I love him and am worried that he might hurt himself ..." The adorable heart of a mother. A heart to be eaten, boiled, with a sprig of rosemary.

24 February—Yuki-chan clearly said PAPÀ, several times. "Mamà" only twice confusedly (7 ½ months).

My adorable mother tenderly regrets that her second daughter whose name in Japanese means "white" and recalls snow, has said

Papà's name several times and hers only twice. Is it possible that at seven months a toddler has already decided to favour one parent over the other? And that she expresses this predilection by calling out her favourite?

It would seem that a form of apprehension about the division of affections naturally arises in all families, however emancipated. "Who do you love best, Papà or me?" What a silly question! Yet it touches raw nerves and burns.

Everything is established in those years, says Elena Gianini Belotti in her book *What Are Little Girls Made Of?: The Roots of Feminine Stereotypes*, a book that was a reference point for women in the 60s.

A tangle of emotional tensions that is difficult to regulate. A father, mother, son, daughter … it seems that nature would do everything. Instead no. Nature would probably push for incest, as happens with animals. "It's one of the first rules of human coexistence, the incest taboo. Malinovski relates this well. It's through exogamy that men have discovered the cultural exchange between different communities, the protection of the group, the division of generations, the distribution of tasks," still shyly whispers my friend, defeated mother in love.

Yuki [...] five times a day drinks cow's milk + 10 gr. Patrogen + 1 apple cooked with sugar and butter + 1 Haliva + mandarin juice + now and then a slice of bread (not often).
26. Yuki says Papà Papà Papà all day long.
9 March. Yuki Cia-ciá—then Da-CIA, she still does not clearly say Mamà!

We have to imagine this Italian family so far from Italy, made up of an intrepid, adventurous father, of a young, resolute mother, extremely exemplified by her role as parent, and three small girls. A fresh pair of parents openly at odds with the aristocratic traditions of entrusting the children to wet nurses, nannies, governesses, even far from home. A usage to which the bourgeois then, by imitation, adopted: Madame Bovary, for example, doesn't think twice about leaving her only daughter in the hands of a crude woman, with absolutely no notion of hygiene. Flaubert, who spies on her from behind a door, judges her severely and follows her when he goes to find his Berthe to the house of Mrs. Roller, the carpenter's wife. "The room in the basement, the only one in the house, had at the end, against a wall, a large bed without curtains: the sideboard occupied the whole wall of the window […] In a corner behind the door, a pair of ankle boots with shiny heels was lined up under the stone sink, next to a bottle full of oil, with a pen tucked inside it.[…] Emma's baby slept on the floor in a wicker cradle. She pulled her up with all the blanket she was wrapped in and began to hum softly, rocking her. Léon walked up and down the room: it seemed strange to him to see that beautiful woman in Nanjing in the middle of such misery. She blushed; he turned away, fearing that he had looked at her impertinently. She hurriedly put down the baby, who had just finished vomiting on her collar. The wet nurse carefully dried it, assuring her that the stain would not be at all visible.

"'I have to clean her constantly,' says the woman, annoyed. And she asks the elegant mother to give her some soap, because she doesn't have money to buy any. 'All right, all right,' Emma hastily responds." And she leaves, drying her feet on the threshold. The poor woman accompanies her to the end of the courtyard, and continues to talk about the fatigue of having to wake up in the middle of the night …"

Not a very tender little portrait, in which Flaubert expresses all his contempt for a selfish and superficial mother. Faced with the desolation of that scene, faced with the filth in which her baby lives, Emma does not show any apprehension, does not show fear, only the annoyance of having her dress stained by the newborn. Flaubert is hard on her. However, he had a very different model in his house. Madame Justine-Caroline Flaubert was so careful and tyrannical that she forced her son to have his girlfriend's letters sent to a friend, so that she would not discover them, and explode in one of her scenes of moralistic maternal jealousy. To note: Flaubert's son was already forty years old.

Here, my mother is the least Bovaryesque person I've ever met. Not at all seduced by the sappy dreams of her time, very concrete in her life plans, very active, she had the attitude of those who say: I'll do it myself because I don't trust others. And often, she was right. After all, she had run away from a Bovary-type mother, yes: her mother Sonia thrived on bad dreams; like Emma Bovary, she was looking for love and fell in love with men who were not to be recommended, and then she complained of heartbreak and suffered, made a great theatre of her suffering. Of course, frustration played its part in the carelessness with which she faced her role as a mother. Having been equipped with a powerful lyric soprano voice and not being able to use it, having a dramatic temperament and not being able to use it on stage, was torture for her. But in those days, a woman from a good family would not go on stage, nor sing in public, except for benefits.

If my grandfather Enrico had not been there, maybe even Sonia, like Emma, would have her daughters with a wet-nurse of a Sicilian farmer in some rural enclave, in the midst of flies and horseflies, leaving herself free to go out on horseback with her lovers. But my grandfather was not Charles Bovary. As well, almost a hundred years had passed since those events.

In her bedroom, Grandmother kept a gigantic photograph of her eye, something that really impressed me when I was a child. An eye as large as a fish, dark, luminous, without expression. I don't know at what age that photo was taken, nor whether my grandmother had cut out the eye from an entire face. In an obscure sign language, that eye lost in the void seemed to express a solitary dismayed cry for help that obviously no one ever listened to. Notwithstanding the love she received from her husband, I think that my grandmother Sonia suffered from nostalgia for the distant land where she was born and raised: Chile. Hers was a life of exile, linguistic and emotional. An exile on whose deepest reasons she had probably never reflected, trapped as she was, in her "bad girl" role, which had become for her almost a source of desperate pride.

While growing up, perhaps my mother had judged too severely that beautiful exuberant woman who could not find peace. That lioness for whom every house was a prison. That voice imprisoned inside a body forced to submit early to the social rules of its class.

To make up for the shortcomings of her seldom-present mother, and to distinguish herself from the passionate Chileans of an ancient family, who although settled in Italy for seventy years, had not yet learned to speak Italian correctly, she had dedicated herself with the meticulous efficiency of a traditional housewife to the care of her daughters.

16 March—D. has tonsillitis again. Fever 39.6. Doctor said she has swollen tonsils. They have to take them out. D. has a terrible earache in one ear—as usual I had to keep my hand on her ear most of the night. She's eaten nothing but mandarin juice.

This image of a young mother who keeps her hand on her daughter's aching ear all night, softly emerges from the nocturnal waters of memory only now, in reading these dry quick words in the diary. Evidently, she was unaware of the sacrifice she was making. No one asked it of her, and so it was more generous. How could a mother and daughter, united by pain, ever be erased from the secret rooms of family reminiscence?

17 March—39—maximum. Bitter medicine in powder form given by doctor (a type of aspirin) and no other cure. Fosco is not here, I'm alone—very upset.
18 March—ditto—half a egg, a bit of milk.
19 March—highest 38—mandarin juice and pineapple.
20 March—Yuki 38—37.6—an egg—biscuits—gave her pyramidone (from Italy) for children. Got up in the morning.
21 March—D. 37.4—Yuki 38.

22 D. and Y. without fever! Slept a lot—pale and thin—she eats a little. Days full of patience, without sleep! More than worried.

In these situations the absence of the father is constant. It was dependent on his work, clearly. But how is it possible that a father would always be far away when his daughter had fever, when she had whooping cough, when she had her first tooth, or on her first day of school? And is it really nature that pushes a mother to keep her hand on her daughter's aching ear all night long?

"Could it be that she wants a career?" is said of a woman who evades these sacrifices, perhaps to follow a job that fascinates her. The word "career" is already a condemnation. As well, in the family, absences in difficult moments are not forgiven, this division of one's self between children and office. If there is no open condemnation, there is mockery. Hundreds of short stories and novels and films and plays and jokes have shown the world how ridiculous or perverse a career woman can be. So much so, that applied to women, this word has become almost useless.

My mother abandoned any aspiration for work when she had me. Yet her painterly hand was light, wise and her paintings, with their bitter and naive traits, still retain an admirable freshness. I have two of her self-portraits that certainly testify to the possibility of her having become a fine painter in the school of Rasai, of Raffaël, of Severini.

She never complained about this interruption of her work. She quit with the enthusiasm illustrated in these notebooks. And no one certainly found that her sacrifice was unfair. Couldn't she have continued to paint and also look after her daughters? Evidently not: the times were not right, the sharing of tasks was not practiced. It was in fact, perfectly normal, for a mother to stifle her talent for her young children. That was that. The husband, instead, was allowed to travel, discover the world, fall in love with other women, and when he returned home, pretend to be welcomed as a king.

The pharmacist precision with which my mother weighed our first poor meals is admirable.

10 January Yuki 6 months—points her feet and can stand if I hold her hands.
Now I'll give her:
8 in the morning 60 grams of cow's milk (boiled).
[...]
12 same as morning with juice of ½ a mandarin.
4 same + a teaspoon of applesauce.
8 same + a Haliva tablet.
12 evening same.
4 A.M. often she wakes and I give her another meal. If she sleeps, she skips this.

Even in this precision I see a contrast to the vague nature of her mother Sonia, who went from resorting to the most extravagant permissiveness, to neglecting the small daily struggles. This young bride committed herself (an almost notarized commitment) to raising her daughters, with a great deal of patience and a didactic will that certainly compensated for her having been completely deprived of both.

At the bottom of the page in the diary, there is glued in newspaper snippet from January 14, 1940. *San Dazio, bishop of Milan from the year 552. B. Odorico Mattiussi da Pordenone (Udine).* To Saint Dazio, I owe my name, handed down in my mother's family as a tribute to the martyr "torn by barbarians" in the 6th Century.

In childhood I hated my name that was too unusual for a little girl. Children, we know, are conformists. They don't understand the pleasure of being different, of differentiating themselves from others, even if it is only with their name. Probably they are still too fragile to venture a position that might alienate them from the norm. My highest aspiration was to not distinguish myself in any way from others, but this was a matter of a pure desire, because I continuously stumbled on my difference: a secular family, precocious travel, the crossing of oceans, a concentration camp experience, hunger, extravagant names: Fosco, Topazia, Yuki, Dacia, all out of the ordinary.

I would have liked to be named Maria, to have been dark haired, with black eyes, to have had two steady parents, a father who went to work every morning, and a fat, reassuring mother. These were the parents of my school mates, be they first in Japan then in Italy. Instead my father was always travelling for his ethnological studies, my mother had the mentality of an eighteen-year-old, in love with us but so dissimilar from the other mothers; in our rooms there were no dolls, paintings of saints, devotional books, but reproductions of Picasso, of Matisse. On the bookcases overflowing with books you could not find romances or useless encyclopaedias, but Proust and Dostoevsky, Virginia Woolf, Henry James and Svevo.

June 1940. D. doesn't want to sleep in the adjoining room. She gets up at night and comes to Mamà, so now she sleeps in the big bed with Mamà (and Papà in the adjoining room). Daciuzza often has earache (left and right) with fever or without.

I wonder if my ears didn't want to reject the noise of the world. Too much noise, too much intensity, too much of too much. Or perhaps, conversely, they heard something distant and threatening that others still did not perceive: a devastating war was approaching that would upset our lives and those of millions.

Now [Yuki] can stand up (supported) for quite a few seconds and doesn't want to talk—she holds out her hand when she wants to be picked up, and kicks furiously. She can sit by herself but falls to the side and it's necessary to put a pillow around her.

And a few days later a huge title on the diary page.

YUKI'S FIRST WORDS

5 July. Almost a year. For the first time Yuki stood up by herself.
Words: Tatta! Odì. Dacia-cìan.
14 July onnicià (Konnichiwa)
Àdà (ya-da)
Babài (banzai) [Long live! A wish for 10,000 years of good health and immortality]
a–bàba (obasan) [the wetnurse]
16 July she learned to give "a little kiss" to Mamà (then quickly unlearned it!)
End of August—she walks well by herself, now and then she loses her balance sideways (funny) and falls, but she doesn't cry.
Beginning of September saonaa (sayonara) goodbye
iraisciaa (irashai) come
pan for any food
oc(i)ta (fallen)
chita (come)
nèe (really?)
na for no, shaking her head
scio da (ciodai) please
End of October abuna (abunai) dangerous
Azì (atsuì) hot

D. loves to read beside Yuki. Both of them in D.'s little bed with the bars, very comfortable, they are very good and very happy. So sweet to look at!

Reading was a fixation. I wanted to read even when I didn't know how to decipher the words and I carried the storybook around, even upside down. I dreamt of being on the flying bed of Little Nemo. It was extraordinary to discover that each time you landed, you ended up in a different country: among fragile giants similar to old-growth trees in which the child became miniscule; among ice houses where the furniture was transparent; among water lilies on whose petals frogs talked and read newspapers: among friendly lions ready to play hide and seek. I was passionate about the events of the Babar elephant family. And then there was Pinocchio who told lies and then ran to his beloved Geppetto.

There were the stories of Mother Goose who laid eggs in the most unexpected places and then had to fight to defend them. There was the family of dwarfs who lived in a gigantic shoe. And the stories of Pierino Procospino, the terrible hedgehog who did not want to get his nails cut, so that they stretched out to the point that they seemed to be the porcupine's spines, or when for fun, he threw flour into the air, which covered him from head to toe, so was put in the oven, "cooked, overcooked and twice cooked," as Goldoni would say. My fantasy had no respite. But I was never satisfied. "Again," I'd say to my mother, "again," until I learned to read and could choose my own books. Even today I become listless and sad if I don't have a story that captures me and takes me by the hand into unknown landscapes, in rooms not mine, in distant and seductive times. I couldn't live without reading.

New Year's 1940

The 31st D. 39.6! at 2, the doctor came: purulent otitis to the middle (right) ear. At 3:00 I took her to Tenchi hospital. At 6 perforation of the eardrum—I was very impressed—they put her to sleep in a minute. In the morning, the fever had lowered. At night, I slept with her in one bed. Fosco in a bed beside us.

For once, my father was there, he must have returned for the holidays.

A good New Year's! On January 2, again a high fever—the other ear! All over as before, out comes a lot of pus, the fever lowers. D. sleeps a lot but won't let go of my hand for even a moment! The dressings are painful and she screams terrified. I end up doing it—so as not to upset her— with the nurse's disapproval. On January 4th 3 degrees fever (tonsillitis) but diphtheria is feared. Quickly they give her the first anti-diphtheria injection—very downhearted, terrible day of anxiety. Day 5 fever starts to lower—it wasn't diphtheria! I'm overjoyed. Everyone is so sweet, they bring candy, flowers, toys. They call. On the 6th we take her home because she is so well that she doesn't want to stay in bed, but I keep her in bed until the 8th, then in her room. The 7th rash all over the body—effects of the anti-diphtheria injection. The 9th her knees are swollen and all the other joints—doctor at first thinks rheumatism, but because there is no fever, decides that it is still the effect of the serum (what a horrid poison!). The 15th she still had hives (for two days) all over her body—like the bites of huge mosquitoes. Poor little girl. She hasn't gone out in 20 days but she doesn't have fever.

There is such apprehension and such tenderness in this mother's bending over the body of her sick daughter to last a lifetime. Had I not been so well nurtured by her affection how could I have endured the concentration camp, the hunger, the worms, the fleas, the bombs, the earthquakes and more hunger, black hunger?

Despite my dramatic view of things, I have a depth of optimism that surely comes from those first great experiences of maternal love.

24 March 1941. D. and Mamà leave Sapporo for Tokyo. Yuki and Papà will join us later with Obasan (5 April).

D. is very interested in meeting so many Italian children—but she hardly speaks! After 40 days in Tokyo, she has already learned a lot of Italian! Everyone finds her so good, so polite. "What a treasure of a child!" With the Japanese children, she is much more naughty, perhaps because she feels at home with them—and they laugh and say "kawaii" no matter what she does! In the hotel, D. befriended everyone. She received gifts from everyone, soldiers, (officers), ladies, waitresses, lift boys! I am extremely mortified!

Strange this transformation. But when did it happen? How did I go from a child who had never been nauseous to a girl who could not even step on a boat without being sick? And when it is that as a sociable little girl, who made friends with soldiers, ladies, waitresses, lift boys I mutated into a very shy girl who could hardly speak, who was afraid to enter a cinema when the lights were on, who feared adults and hovered in corners so as not to be seen? I can't find the breaking point, that crack from which my character suddenly began to fall apart.

Japanese children with whom I was naughty I don't recall. I recall instead my mother, her kind intelligence I felt was threatened by wounds and injuries. I had a terrible fear of losing her. Young, her blonde hair long and fine, her body, soft, scented. I thought everyone wanted to steal her away. I couldn't sleep until I heard her return, lean over me for a last kiss. Her blue eyes, tender, scrutinized me in the dark; I pretended to sleep and breathed in her scent of lipstick, of hair sprayed with rose water, of heat, of sake just drunk. Sometimes, I would hug her and say, "Please stay." She, patient, would put her purse on the floor, sit on the bed, and would sing the chorus from *Madama Butterfly* that even today makes a lump in my throat.

D. begins to speak in the Kyoto dialect (pronounced like Florentine). The only disadvantage of this house—the "tonari," the neighbours with five dirty, rude children with whom D. always wants to play. It's a struggle to keep her at home because of Japanese customs; the children come here.

I don't recall those games, but I do remember the taste of bitter, smoky air. Occasionally a mother would appear to call one of the children: Mieko chan! Yunichiro chan! And immediately you could hear the patter of the zori, the raffia sandals that scraped along the sidewalk. A dog barking. A chorus of girls emerging from the nearby school. The scent of blanched daikon and freshly steamed rice. I felt myself to be as Japanese as those other snot-nosed children, who ran and called each other from the most bizarre hiding places. What is diversity then, a feeling? A wall of flesh? A concoction of recognizable smells? I don't know even today.

5 April 1941. We are all in Kyoto.
We arrived in time for the famous (justifiably) Cherry Blossom. Together we visit the Heian Jingu, Shinto temple.

Much later I learned the meaning of Shinto. A generous archaic faith that gives language to the dead, plants and animals, that believes in heroes and wars, in loyalty at the cost of life and in the language of ghosts.

The Japanese skilfully mixed the old religion of the goddess Amaterasu, the spirits and the infallible emperor, with the new more abstract and philosophical one of the spiritual rules of Buddha which arrived four times from China in the 6th century, through the Korean monks who first introduced the books of the Sutra.

I remember a delightful watercolour that narrates with some malice the wreck of a boat that shuttled between the Chinese and Japanese coasts centuries ago during the religious transmigration. The wood slips and slides, leaps and falls awkwardly on the blue and green curls of a stormy sea. Inside the boat a dozen Korean monks are agitated and frightened to discover their arms and legs now immersed in the raging water. One tries to catch his hat that a gust of wind has blown away, another tries with a saucepan to collect water that enters copiously from the sides of the boat, a third tries desperately to maneuver the oars that tend to be dragged into the current. Two monks with bare arms and legs are intent on dumping the ballast overboard, and among the heaviest things are sacred books. Only one, a young man, who we guess to be particularly pious, desperately watches the open volumes, blowing in the wind, which recede, pushed by the waves.

It is not that the two religions, so different, had an easy convergence, almost an arranged marriage. Two countries that had much trade, much business even literary, could not fail to draw from each other's religious practices. It was a matter of facing a laborious war that dragged on for years, between the powerful priestly families of the Makatoni and the Mononobe committed to defending the ancient religion of their ancestors, and the large and modern Soga family that supported and protected Buddhism. At the beginning the change mainly concerned intellectuals, artists and philosophers, who saw Buddhism as a modern and reflective religion, less fetishistically attached to things. Only at the end of the 8th century did the poor, the peasants and the fishermen also begin to approach the slightly nihilistic spirituality of Buddhism. This is always how clever, very intelligent syncretism arises, always ready to keep the best of an ancient tradition, mixing it with the modernity of a bursting new universalist doctrine. But the real transformation of the Chinese religious philosophy into a widespread religion across all levels of the Japanese population arrived with Zen Buddhism in the 12th Century.

Touring around today's Japan, I have noted in many houses, be they of the wealthy or the poor, the presence to one side, of an altar where one honours the ancestors, offering them fresh rice balls with *Tsukemono*, small cups of sake, sweets of yokan, soy pasta. On the other hand, these houses never lack a small niche for the sober and kind image of Buddha, who disdains food and smiles a little ironically at these archaic habits. His wise body, seated in the lotus flower pose, teaches that human life is an illusion, that true wisdom consists in detaching oneself from desires and passions, to devote oneself to fasting and meditation.

In short, even now, in the era of big banks and electronic com-munications, just like before and during the Second World War, the dead in Japanese homes circulate among the living with a benevo-lent and affectionate spirit. At night they nibble a little of that food offered devoutly: they move without making noise, in their 'tabi,' ankle socks in spotless cotton, and shake their heads thoughtfully when things are not going well in the family, and smile instead when life flows calmly.

All this under the indulgent eye of the Buddha who, although he preaches justice, honesty, and respect for all living creatures, main-tains a practice of detachment from material things of the world, a kind of "from dust to dust" that we understand well. However, the awareness of Buddhist nothingness is sweeter and more nuanced. Man can, through a series of bad choices live a hundred lives, as a man or as a cockroach, as a queen or a sow, but in the end he will reach Nirvana and know the perfection of the universe. The idea of rebirth is consoling and sweetens the waiting time for the Christian dead, before they leave the grave to the sound of the trumpets of Judgment.

The reasoning, certainly, came later but the physical experience of that Cherry Blossom Festival is present in my memory—sometimes it even seems ready and elastic, other times instead completely spent and inert. I find myself breathless for a word, groping in the darkness of a memory that is aging. Often along with the word escapes the very meaning of experience. There, where there is no name, as Wittgenstein says, there is nothing. Is this true? And how to demonstrate it?

The "Momigi"—maples—had changed colour. The slightest flutter of leaves ranging from ocher to amaranth, from pink gladiolus to egg yellow. Years later I assisted in a Nō play where an old tree narrated its past. It was actually a maple, I seem to remember, that at the moment of the color mutation, recovered the word and addressed the wayfarers with a wise intelligent voice.

The Zeami texts have taught me that plays are also put on to evoke the dead, who are not enemies to nail inside coffins, as the Catholic tradition suggests. Mysterious beings may come out of the graves to the sound of the trumpets of Judgment but how will they come out? In the form of shining youths or rotting corpses, as the numerous films on the living dead propose? In Japanese culture the dead are not threatening, don't have canine teeth ready to sink into the necks of the naïve, but they present themselves like friends, preoccupied with questions of honour, with whom one can converse in the nights of the full moon.

I recall that on that day of the festival at the Shinto temple of Heian, standing in the crowd, I thought for the first time of the world as an ensemble of people, each one with her mother, with her own coloured kimono, with her own shoes, with her own toys, with her own omochi. It was a strange, disturbing thought. Perhaps it was my first glimmering reflection on otherness. There were many me's besides me, and all unknown. What kept them together? And why did they walk in the same direction? Who could tell them how and when to go? When to come back? How to dress? How to eat? What to think? Who were those children who resembled me, yet were so different?

Perhaps I had also heard Mamà and Papà talking about the rising Nazism and the impending war, even if we had not yet tasted its bitter fruits.

I wasn't even six years old and my father would say, "Remember that races do not exist. There are different cultures but races do not exist." And this right at the moment when all of Europe was in the grip of a racist exaltation. To which he reacted with stubborn and decisive refusal, for which many rebuked him.

Now and then Mamà takes the sisters "machini" (in the city). Program: Dari Moi department store, toys. Yuki can never understand herself what she wants. D. doesn't want anything! (very blasé). She's always search-ing for something very new, something that's never been seen, exciting and then ends up wanting to buy a pencil sharpener or a coloured hand-kerchief or a useless plastic trinket.

Then ice-cream—then we return home in the bus—tired, satisfied.

The curious thing is that still today I love pencil sharpeners and coloured handkerchiefs. In the department stores or in the Sunday markets, I look at everything but I end up focusing my attention on a cotton or silk scarf, possibly blue. Blue is my colour, what gives me peace when I am uneasy. Reading Flaubert I discovered that he also loved blue, a colour to which he attributed erotic powers. Usually red matches sensuality. And instead, every time Emma Bovary gets ready to make love there is something cerulean that transfigures her: The veil that flows from her hat when she goes out on horse-back in the woods with Rudolphe, the merino wool suit with the blue flounces, the turquoise walls of a hotel room. Even Emma's eyes, that Flaubert says are black, become, in the passion of love, a splendid sapphire blue.

In the magnificent garden of Gin Kakuji, while Mamà takes part in a tea ceremony, the girls drink ritual green tea in the kitchen—then they run on the moss with bare feet. They would stay there all day.

It's a small family portrait. One that will repeat for years. Papà is there but is not there. Mamà tries to sink into the local customs: we wear kimonos, evident in many photographs, with the obi high to hold together the slippery edges of silk. We participate in the popular Japanese celebrations. We drink bitter green tea, which is often accompanied by small rice sweets and yokan made with a dark and sugary paste. We learn the language or rather the dialect. We play with Japanese children. The nannies are all local, and I speak Japanese much better than Italian. If this isn't integration! And it was not a duty, but a pleasure of mind and body. Except that it is difficult to establish the limits between one culture and another. And what if, by practicing different customs, you lose the ancient knowledge of yourself? If leaving one language and insinuating yourself into another, do you lose the connections on which your semantic logic rests? These are the difficulties that every emigrant encounters, even if only for foreign study, even if not pressed by misery and hunger.

What effect did the sometimes contradictory teachings of two civilizations so distant and unknown to each other have on a turbulent, sensible child? It's difficult to tell. I had moments when I thought I was losing my mind, as we say. But then I recovered. Mounting difficulties either destroy you or induce you to build survival strategies, even joyful, even ingenious ones. I entrusted myself to instinct and instinct was able to navigate the waves, the harshest ones. In the world of symbols I don't suffer from seasickness, like I did when I was a one-year-old voyaging on the Conte Verde.

Can one fall in love with the past? *Longing*, as my mother would say in English. *Longing for the past.* The past that appears under my eyes in these photographs, fixed and forever glossy, is as seductive as a Medusa. While the present is rough and thorny, almost revolting in its bareness.

But what is the moment when the present is irreparably transformed into the past? The moment after is the logical answer. But after what? After the moment we are living? Yet if we dwell on that moment, it no longer exists, we cannot analyze it because it has disappeared into thin air. Could it be that time is an idea we create out of something that doesn't exist? An arbitrary abstraction that we construct in our image and likeness and to whom we give fictitious names in the desperate attempt to detain it, to give it form? Memories are actually filled with names and those guarantee to us that something has happened. But what? The photographs presume to tell us with precision. They present themselves as the most reliable witnesses of memory linked to images. Despite this, I always had the impression that the images are there to fool us. With authority and privilege they reveal reality, even as they embellish it, glaze it, render it two-dimensional and absolutely only paper.

Now and then, D. speaks Italian! Very funny, with Japanese syntax.

One day, Papà gave her "tetelle" and she was indignant, "Papà, brutta l'uomo!7"

It's still the 12th of April 1940; D. says, "Mamà questo a Dacia non ti piace" and speaks Italian with Japanese grammar rules. Hilarious!

A linguistic duplicity that has certainly magnified my expressive insecurity to the point of making it persistent. I've always solved things with writing. It was easier for me to write than to speak. I had a lot of difficulty with the bodies of the people I had to address. An obsessive and paralysing form of shyness. The individual who stood in front of me, be it friend, however well-intentioned, plastered the words in my mouth. If instead I sat down, even on the

---

7   D.'s sentences are grammatically incorrect in Italian.

steps of the metro and wrote ten words on a sheet of squared paper torn from a school notebook, I felt more free.

Writing is certainly a passion that comes from my paternal side: my grandmother Yoi wrote delightful travel books. My father has always written and continues to write with such an effervescent style! Italian after a few setbacks, has become my language. But I am familiar with linguistic transmigrations, a la Conrad. Maybe this is also a reason why I love him so much. It was a joy for me to translate *Il Compagno segreto (The Secret Sharer)*. Whose title now, with more courage, I would change to *A Stowaway On Board*, which instead I chose as the title of my book of reflections. The fact is that *The Secret Sharer* is not translatable. There is no equivalent to the word *sharer* in Italian. But how hard it is to decipher such a difficult and complex language, with a layered and unnatural structure! Working on it one understands that it is an adopted language, made so through hard work. But perhaps precisely for this reason his narrative body of work, marked by wounds, by buried angers, by feelings of guilt, by continuous tests and experiments, becomes so seductive, absolutely lovable.

137

Papà went to Tokyo—in the evening Mamà and D. go together for a walk along the solitary roads to enjoy what little fresh air there is. D. darling! Wants to know so many things and speaks often of the kodomo that will be born and that for now is inside the honourable tummy of Mamà.

Curious this continual need to take a backward step, to put oneself aside and look at the mother and child who walk after supper in search of some fresh air. "Mamà and Dacia" does not indicate solitude, abandonment, but a perfect loving symmetry. Actually, we were not two, on the contrary three, or better still four with the little Toni who was sleeping curled in Mamà's tummy, awaiting her turn to come into the world. Many questions remained under the tongue of a precocious and embarrassed little girl. Where do children come from? Yes, I knew they were in the maternal tummy, but before, who decided whether they should be born or not, and when did that little body take shape, which would later be recognizable like that of my honourable sister?

Another girl? my father would have said, disgusted. While not being misogynous, he wanted a boy who would carry his name and continue the family traditions. From male to male, the handover is always the same. There are mysteries, my friend Giovanni would say, that are handed down from father to son, there are affinities, carnal similarities that the mother cannot understand. But is it really like this, dear Giovanni? Is it not rather that in that arcane lineage what is handed down is the secret of male domination?

The girl in question showed a desire for autonomy that would be foolish to think does not belong to the feminine nature, even if in contradiction with the commonplace beliefs about girls of all times.

D. immediately wanted to go out and explore the surroundings. The children in the neighbourhood laughed then ran, almost frightened of the "mezurashi" apparition of a living "o ningh-yo-san" (doll). D. instead of being distressed, ran after them with a string of Japanese sentences that had the desired effect. After 20 minutes, they were all around her (10–15!) and after an hour, they played and chased each other in the garden or on the street, and in the little courtyards of the houses "tonari." Now when she comes home from school at 1, she takes off her coat and runs immediately to the "tomodachi." In the evening she returns when it's dark—sweaty she is hungry and sleeps well—now in a big bed alone in the room next to ours, with Yuki chan in the adjacent crib.

They both awaken in the morning at 6 much to my great desperation. L'obasan comes at 7 so I return to sleep for a bit.

In Rancima, D. wanted to walk "lontano, lontano, itari no ho made"8. D. has a boy friend who is about eight years old. "Last year I died," she said (who knows what she meant?). And he said, "No, silly, last year you were born!"

---

8   *"Far, far, to the end"*—half in Italian, half in Japanese.

More under the title "hilarious conversations."

D.: Mamà (in Japanese) you are very good when you speak Italian, English and French, but you're so funny when you speak Japanese—you have to ask me how to say it!

And more: *After the party for her birthday, I ask D. which child is her favourite. Rudy (Fachtman), she says, because he likes to wrestle (and we at first were afraid that they were really fighting during their wrestling)!*

February '41: "Mamà, we mustn't take too much stuff to Itarì or the boat will be too heavy and will go down down down and then capsize. As well, if Yuki chan moves, I who am the nesan will hold on to her so she doesn't fall in the sea and drown. Remember, okay?"

3 August. [...] Papà often takes Dacina swimming—seated on a little chair hanging on his bicycle. D. is happy. D. adores doing "abunai" things, like her father.

Abunai means prohibited, difficult. In short, a reckless daredevil. I have memories of some years later in Bagheria, when I hurled myself down steep, unpaved roads on my father's bicycle. And because I couldn't reach the saddle, I pedalled with one leg inserted in the triangle that joins the rod to the wheel. I fell a hundred times, I grazed my knees, I injured myself, but I didn't stop rushing down on the bicycle whose brakes only worked in fits and starts.

On summer days, I dipped my head into the water that exploded into the air from a protruding rock, risking being smashed. You had to choose the exact moment, when the wave instead of hitting you, welcomed you into itself. Woe if you were afraid.

So, to pick the cherries or locust beans, I climbed the tallest plants, defying the birds and even there, however much I happened on old rotten branches, I never fell or really was hurt. And what about the game we played with Yuki, Toni and little Japanese friends: we waited for a car, then ran across the road before it could run us over. Whoever reached the opposite sidewalk at the moment closest to the arrival of the car won. The driver braked, frightened, then left sounding his horn, indignantly.

How cute they are, comments my mother, in front of a photograph in which my father is sitting on top of a rock, in a bathing suit, and I am standing next to him, wearing a full skirt and a round straw hat. Was there a sense of exclusion in that "cute"? However, she would have been right, because those are the years of my great love for my father, the Triton, the unrepentant seducer, the heartbreaker, the Peter Pan who flew out the window in the evening, to who knows which countries, with intense smells and bright colours. "Papà, when are you coming back?" "Soon, Dacina, soon." And that soon was like a never. Because it triggered the difficult feeling of waiting, and the waits, we know, are snakes that tangle into our sleeping minds.

11 August to 19 August we stayed in a cabin on Mount Hiei, but it rained the whole time—and it was almost too cold and uncomfortable for the girls—we returned to the city: terrible heat that gave Yuki a cough.

My father has always flaunted a resounding contempt for comfort and considered it 'gentleman-with-hat' nonsense. A person with the right heart did not seek comfort and unnecessary luxuries, but slept on hard ground, inside a tent, on a mountain peak; he ate frugally and never complained. So his daughter had to behave like the brave child he loved: an accomplice to an austere and monastic ideal of life. Money doesn't matter, property doesn't count, social talk less than ever. Instead, the harmony of our relationship with things matters: Fish in the midst of fish, bird in the midst of birds, the free body must be ready to follow the traces of an entirely secular and naturalistic path towards the conquest of serenity.

Papà and Dacia as usual are playing together.

We are on a wide wooden plank that slides on the waters of a lake. This was exactly what made me fall in love with him: the absolute inability to dramatize, which my mother had instead. The joyful, unconscious bravado of his being in the world, secure and natural, courageous and adventurous. How can we fail to admire a beautiful young man who walks on the edge of life and at moments dances, without taking into account the abysses that open beneath him, without fear of slipping, of losing his balance? On that edge, he was also capable of eating, drinking, sleeping and inventing an absurd poem on the sweetness of aunts:

Oh aunts oh sweet aunts in *bardocheta*
turn within the embroidered *glime*
descend the stairs *beta beta*
from the *maberi* of fused time!
Who knows if down there the *sobite*
Slowly *gramugna* in *cantalaghi*
in the *ufe coccia ccoccia* of the night?
Now it's no use going out on the *sbaghi*
staring ahead with haughty air,
among the *lugheri,* the *archostoli,* the *snaghi.*9

The war had already exploded, it was claiming victims all over Europe, but in our small family garden, the voices of discord and violence did not reach us. Family happiness, one might say, loves to feed on itself, and builds walls around its own well-being.

I loved, waited and searched for that Peter Pan who was my father, with whom I went so willingly to explore the world. He was a tribal chief always ready to leave, to discover new streams, new craggy rocks on which to climb, new woods to search, new deserts to cross. Without compass, without water. Carrying only a small

---

9   In Italian, a metalanguage of assonances and inventions; a linguistic game full of deep echoes.

rucksack on his back, which contained a tiny apple to divide in two, crampons, a rope, binoculars and a book.

7–17 September Mamà and Papà in Tokyo. The girls are in Kyoto. From Tokyo I phone them often. Yuki at the phone: "Mocci Mocci, natta oidé, né?" and Dacia tells me she is being very good and could I bring her a little gift!

The culture of gifts had made its victims … Even now I cannot escape the logic of offerings made to appease the mysterious souls of strangers.

Overnight Yuki developed a high fever—difficulty breathing. Terrified it's diphtheria, but it isn't. 40.2. It's tonsillitis. She's fine by the 22nd.

Strange this obsessive fear of diphtheria, which did promptly show up in our house, but not till we'd returned to Italy, in Bagheria. And I remember perfectly the comings and goings of my mother with food, in a dish covered by a net. My sister Toni and I could only see her from a window. We were not allowed to enter that room on the ground floor of Villa Valguarnera where Yuki lay, ashen and alone in a cot. We had just returned from Japan. Still thin and weakened by the detention. And Yuki one day complained of a sore throat. Fortunately, my mother had waged a fierce war against diphtheria. She had so hated it, that it had come, but was immediately stopped at the threshold: "You will not enter here!" Although it had already infected the weaker sister, it absolutely had no need to touch the other two. And rolling up her sleeves, showing an absolute contempt for the infection, she entered and left the patient's room, sparing the nanny, who would have liked to have helped her. She was not afraid of disease, and like a lioness had decided to snatch her second-born from death.

And in the end, she was successful. Through medicines, lemons, disinfected hot water, and caresses. The diphtheria snuck sway, tail between its legs, and never returned. Although my mother, every now and then, peered into our throats in search of those white plaques that she feared like the plague. "Show me, open your mouth." And we there, like three little birds waiting for the mother's beak.

Exactly those little birds, possibly sparrows, that I had tried to sculpt in clay while I was at the boarding school in Florence. I don't know how, I was accused of stealing a clay ball from a schoolmate. An absolutely unfair accusation that I felt like a whip in my face, and whose pain I have never forgotten. No one had ever said, "Don't steal!" It was the most natural thing in the world. It wasn't a rule imposed from above, but a practice that was part of our daily lives. And that accusation had really upset me. How could they even think that I would steal that clay?

Once in Centocelle, where I was mounting a play, I saw an actor who had scattered a pile of very expensive new books on the ground. "Who knows how much you spent!" I said.

"Nothing," he replied, slyly. "I took them from a bookstore without paying."

"You stole them?"

"No, it was a proletarian expropriation. Aren't we proletarians?"

It really didn't seem so to me. He was the son of a lawyer and even though he lived in a basement suite, because his father did not give him money, he was always a young man from a good family, used to all the comforts.

But did ideology really allow me to overturn the rules with which I was raised? Did believing in a radical change in the world authorize you to leave the contract established with your contemporaries, with your fellow citizens? I struggled. On the one hand, I wanted to participate fully in the euphoria of change: the great plans for a future that would end injustices, and brutalities of one class on the other. But at the same time I found it difficult to reverse the elementary rules on which I had built my peace of conscience: not to steal, not to kill, not to lie. Instead, in 1968, suddenly it seemed that everything was possible and reversible. Stealing was a right, killing too, if it was done for a just cause. Even if this latter right wasn't put into practice by anyone I knew, there was the idea that it was legitimate to stamp your feet, to chop off toes, to beat an innocent man bloody, to shoot at someone's legs if he did not think like you: new morality for new world views. I was distressed. Luckily. I have always had some resistance to fanaticism, whatever faith it was. And this reluctance I think saved me from throwing myself into the fray with my peers thirsting for civil wars.

24 September 1941. Yuki-chan went to Yochien for the first time. D. acts like a little mother. All amazed and moved. D. has become truly wise and so reasonable and sensible—more grown up.

I don't know where this judgement came from. Perhaps it was simply a reflection from my mother's bosom. In a photo from that period, we can insinuate the theatre we had constructed to express our sensibility: a large French door that opens onto the garden, a wicker table, an upholstered armchair. My mother, young and wise, with her dress of light dots on a dark background, her hair gathered at the nape of her neck, sits on a wicker armchair, her legs under the table. She wears a serious expression, concentrated and intent on a job that we do not exactly understand: is she going to fill a basket with packages, or is she placing food and tea cups on the table? On the ground an open book awaits to be picked back up. Opposite we see the sensible girl who helps her mother to set the table. Dressed in light clothing, she wears flat shoes, her hair is cut short or she looks thoughtful: which box to remove first from the table?

The photo takes me, across the mysterious roads of literary memory, to Murasaki Shikibù, as I've known her in my imagination, in the process of writing with her paintbrush on a large sheet of rice paper. Her novel may possibly be the most complete and best means to understand Japan. In retrospect, of course, after having breathed its humid air for a long time and drunk its perfumed tea one thousand times. How to forget the story of Prince Genji:

a young and seductive man, who everyone fell in love with just by looking at him. The slender and kind young man whom the courtesans spied from behind curtains, while seated on the large terraces that open along the low wooden houses.

Funny the story of this exquisite Japanese female writer: in the year 1000 in Japan the literati wrote only in Chinese, because that was the language of the learned, of the poets, of the philosophers. The Japanese, like our vernacular, was left to women, to servants. And Murasaki Shikibù, a small woman of court with fluid thoughts and an attentive gaze, made noble the language of the inferiors, composing the most beautiful novel in Japanese literature.

Countries, I'm convinced, are understood mostly through novels. They carry you into secret rooms and corridors of distant houses, in unknown cities. They put in your mouth tastes of soups you've never tasted; they make you touch the contour of muscles in the bodies of friends and enemies; they delight us with a song of a wet nurse or with the sensual softness of an afternoon nap.

How many exquisite and mysterious things I've known of Japan through the enchanted detachment of Kawabata, the erotic complications of Tanizaki, the desperate heroisms of Mishima, the troubled tenderness of Inoue, the secret visions of Hayashi Fumiko.

As for my propensity to mother my sisters, I simply repeated my mother's affectionate gestures. Once again, the example was essential for the formation of a "wise little woman." Without taking into account, however, that that wisdom could also become a trap to fall into. I don't know how far it was in my case. Of course every example can turn into a too-tight dress when the limbs stretch and widen. But unstitched, stretched, with patches or not, I still wear that dress and I've become accustomed to it.

An artificial lake near Kyoto, water cold, deep, writes my mother. At the centre of concentric circles, you see my adored Papà, who comes out of the muddy water only with his head. Hanging on to his shoulders, with her arms around his neck, is a blonde girl with a grave look. A little frog climbing on the back of the large father frog. The adult body drags the child's body through the whirlpools and brings it safely on the shore. From any adventure the two of us came out each time amazed and unharmed. Wasn't it the miracle of a father's love for his little girl and a little girl's for her very young Papà?

We could have fallen, smashed our heads, injured ourselves: while driving like the wind on a silver motorcycle, while we climbed on steep rocks, while we descended precipitously between the stones of a path overlooking a cliff, while swimming under water with oxygen cylinders attached to our backs, while we caracoled our bicycles on dirt paths. But instead, it never happened. His recklessness seemed to protect us better than a guardian angel. We were launched towards the infinite possibilities of adventure. No one could stop us. Least of all caution. "A father and daughter, there they are," almost not speaking to each other. But they found themselves shoulder-to-shoulder pitching the tent on wind-beaten ground; they discovered themselves clinging to each other while facing the overwhelming currents of a river, face-to-face while devouring a piece of bread with cheese under an improvised canopy, caught by a sudden rain in the middle of a more dangerous and exhilarating expedition than the last one. Always in search of something difficult to track down: the path of treasure, the shore of hope, the meadow of peace, the boat of happiness.

Sometimes I realize that he was treating me like a son, forgetting my girlish fragility, the age of my female growing body. Not having had the son he wanted, he thought perhaps of transforming me into the little boy companion of his adventures. For my part, I did my best to not disappoint him at any cost. I had to show myself to be at the height of his expectations, whether I be male or female. I climbed, clenching my teeth even when I was tired, walked for kilometres without ever dragging my feet. I threw myself into the frozen waters of rivers without breathing a word, even though I didn't know how to swim. His education consisted of a Spartan spurring me to independence. I throw you in the water and you swim!

And in fact, I did learn how to swim, without lessons, without training, just to survive. Certainly, had I begun to swallow water, he would have come to my aid. He didn't want me to drown. But he thought, stoically, that faced with difficulty, one sharpens one's skills. And I must say that my survival skills have not remained inert. I learned the lesson.

The big risky trips belonged to Papà and me. Mamà was at home looking after the honourable tummy from which the third sister would soon be born. The second, Yuki, was often sick and my mother cared for her with her usual tenacious passion.

So we were left alone in our enterprise of explorers and pioneers. Impulses that I believe he credited to his grandmother Yoi who, young and beautiful, did not hesitate for a moment to abandon her husband and two children to go on an adventure alone. A restless, solitary, courageous woman whom my father worshipped. Always clashing with grandfather Antonio who wanted him to cede to reason, to stability, to well-paid professionalism, to political acquiescence. It is no coincidence that, when my father got married, my grandfather gave him a Fascist membership card, and that my father tore that card into a thousand pieces. After that they never spoke again for fifteen years.

His escape to Japan had also been an escape from his father. He hoped to convince his mother to visit him, once he was established there, and maybe to convince her to remain with him for the rest of her life.

This story is similar to the one that Natalia Ginzburg tells so well in her fabulous book on the Manzoni family. Alessandro's mother, Giulia Beccaria, had abandoned the severe and dull husband Pietro, and had gone to Paris with Carlo Imbonati, painfully leaving behind the young son her husband had not wanted to entrust to her. For years, the child Alessandro was no longer allowed even to pronounce his mother's name. "When you come of age you will decide whether to see her or not ..." In fact, as soon as he turned twenty, the young Alessandro left for Paris. There he discovered a young, beautiful, intelligent and witty woman, and decided to live with her, then taking her to Milan and keeping her close to him until her death.

My father would have liked to have done a similar thing. But the war prevented him. That war that brooded under the ashes of our adventures on land and water, under our happy carefree partnership.

Another photograph finds us near the Asahigawa river. It was September 10, 1941. In that year, Nazi Germany invaded Bulgaria, Yugoslavia and Greece. In December, our beloved host country bombed Pearl Harbour. The United States and Great Britain declared war on Japan.

Meanwhile, the country of the Order of the Rising Sun—as if fixated on its politics of great power, and imperturbable in the face of the now more and more frequent defeats—occupies Thailand, invades the Philippines and Malaysia, subdues Hong Kong and its international port. Meanwhile Hitler systematically gives the go-ahead to his "Final Solution."

Was it possible that none of this pandemonium leaked into the small Maraini family? Could it be that we remained so happily and blatantly immune to hostilities? Or was there a tenacious and stubborn will on my mother's part to keep us out, at all costs, out of that dirty business?

I asked her and she told me that the culture in Kyoto at the time was very closed. "Nothing could be said that was political. There was censorship on every form of thought and word and the Italians were kept under constant observation." What is certain is that we settled gracefully in the silence of a tense peace that proceeds to war. There were no signs of nervousness and excessive fears for the future. It is also probable that my parents spoke to each other without letting me know anything, so as not to alarm me.

It will still take two years for the spell to brutally break. Before they come to pick us up to take us to the Nagoya concentration camp, together with ten other men, the only non-military

Italians from all over Japan, who did not want to sign the Republic of Salò.[10]

While Yuki chan sleeps on the soft delightful futon in the Shimizu house, Papà, Mamà and Dacia go out to the country with their Shimizu friends, eating delicious melons, grasping dragonflies and finally they have a magnificent dip in the river near the farm—a magnificent day of hot sun and rice almost mature.

At the beginning of 1942, Japan invades Burma, and Singapore surrenders. I recently saw a documentary on the taking of Singapore from the Japanese point of view: atrocious for the use of systematic torture, rape, violence against civilians. Perhaps precisely because they felt the breath of defeat at their necks, they had become more fierce and ruthless. Or perhaps because the war, which has now been full for three years, had made them embittered. Thousands died, even among Japanese soldiers.

I cannot help but think back to that beautiful episode of the Kurosawa film in which an officer is unable to free himself from his soldiers who chase him wherever he goes, with their poor equipment: dirty woolen bands around their legs, shoes gaping and broken from too much walking, backpacks beating against bony shoulders, overloaded with pots and tin cans. The officer turns and shouts to them: "The war is over, just go home, go home!" The soldiers observe him for a moment, lost, and then continue, undaunted, to follow him.

On closer inspection, they have strange, startled faces. They are as white as paper and their eyes seem not to see. At the nth order to go home, they stop for a moment obediently and then resume pathetic trudging behind their commander as if they do not know, even if they want to, other paths. And that's when we discover with horror that they are all dead.

---

10   A satellite state of Nazi Germany during the later part of World War II (from 1943 until 1945). It was the second and last incarnation of the Fascist Italian state and it was led by Duce Benito Mussolini and his reformed Republican Fascist Party.

Meanwhile, the list of illnesses lengthens.

D.: 20 June—ear ache l.r. No fever.
3 July. 38.8—ear ache r. next day 37.2
End of July—light dysentery—Biogermina—excellent
Beginning Sept. cold—cough without fever. Codeine.
9 Sept. without pain r. ear
12 Oct. fever—ear ache r.l. and tonsilles + cough
13 Oct. to 22—high fever 39-40 intermittent, tonsillitis (doctor qui-
nine injection)
1-2 November—38—ear ache l. because she played outside till late! [...]
3 Nov. All well.
Yuki
July 21: few fever lines—bad temper—disappearing. Red and swollen
gums. Night 2 upper front teeth cut through.
22: light diet—milk toast rice water—mandarin juice (2 candies!) tem-
perature 37 and had two bowel movements but not good.
No fever—happy—no bowel movement
24: morning did not poo, in the afternoon 4 times loose, no fever, in the
evening lumpy and yellow. 37.9
25—one bowel movement, greenish, lumpy. At 4 p.m. took her to hosp.
Dr. Nagai. Diet: rice water and milk (half and half) + 2 blended raw
apples + medicine (pepsin, etc.) 37.2 whiny.
26—27 twice p. yellow and lumpy. Better mood but weak and thin.
26 midnight—after a big sweat, temperature 35.6—cold hands,
pale, whimpering—great fear—perhaps too much medicine (stupid!).
Wrapped in blankets, after a while regained her colour!
27—twice p. morning and night around 8:00 yellow and frothy—
identical to yesterday (I didn't give her medicine) good mood—same
diet—temp. 36.4
28 morning early p. ugly same. Changed diet (my invention).
1st meal rice water (a pinch of Biogermina)
2nd meal yoghurt 50 gr. With 3 teaspoons of sugar and 3 light biscuits.
3rd and 4th meals like 1st and 2nd.
Evening no p. no temp.

29—morning p. much better. Banzai! I'm continuing the same diet as yesterday, good mood and stronger. Stood up.
30/31—good. Slowly added biscuits and toast.

The pages preceding the deterioration of the war situation are full of meticulous observations on our feces, on our saliva. Infant fever seemed to signify something, perhaps an alarm for what was to come. But it was too cryptic and mysterious a language even for my very loving mother.

A mother who, meanwhile, inserts a tuft of Yukiko's hair between the pages of the diary. Could it be that she didn't feel the storm gathering over our heads? It seemed our intestines were more alarmed than the consciousness of our beloved parents.

Certainly they couldn't know that in those very days, from all of Europe departed trains crammed with thousands and thousands of Jewish families, men women and children, even newborns, towards the German and Polish troop trains. Back then nobody was aware. And when two Jewish prisoners, fortunately escaped from the Auschwitz camp, told the English authorities what was going on in those torture and death centres, they didn't want to, they couldn't believe. And Pope Pius XII, to whom information from German Catholics was constantly arriving, did not give credit to their words and did not want to say anything against the Nazi deportation.

We now know: in front of us are photos of those children who descended the trains, still in their best clothes, well nourished, even though they had passed days and days without food and water inside a crowded railcar. They jumped down happily to go outside, to be able to quench their thirst, and did not imagine that they would be killed immediately. In fact, children were not useful for ammunition factories and therefore had to be eliminated as soon as possible. They were made to undress, sometimes accompanied by mothers, to keep them quiet: "Hang your clothes on those hooks and remember the number, so afterwards you won't waste time looking for them," kindly suggested a female S.S. officer, pushing them towards the entrance of the gas chamber.

It took years of experiments to discover the effectiveness of the lethal gas Zyklon B. The Germans had tried with the exhaust system of trucks, diverting the flow of the outlet pipe inwards, and so they killed hundreds, but the system was not adequate: death occurred too slowly. The people inside the truck vomited, shouted, threw themselves against the walls, and the screams sometimes travelled too far, alarming the other prisoners. Another method had to be invented. The elimination had to take place, according to Himmler's indications, in absolute secrecy. Nobody had to guess the fate that awaited him. The safest and easiest solution, the orders from Berlin said, was to keep people arriving from ghettos in ignorance: with polite ways they had to be convinced to enter the gas chambers as quickly as possible, persuaded to go for a shower. Above all, it was necessary to prevent even a single word from being exchanged with the other prisoners. In fact, almost everyone in the camp knew about that end, but they kept the secret, out of fear but also perhaps out of a form of pity towards those poor defenseless beings. A survivor told that once, on seeing a woman he knew in the row in front of the gas chamber, whispered, at the risk of his life: "Be careful, they are sending you all to your death." But she had not believed him and had shown him soap, as the most tangible proof of entering a shower room.

The efficient organization of the camps had also experimented with mass shootings. However, they proved to be dangerous, because those who waited or knew their fate tried to rebel or passively resist. The S.S. had to be alert, their nerves tense for the duration of the executions, in which they were forced to keep so many soldiers ready to shoot on the spot. A waste of time and energy. Despite this, it had happened that sometimes the prisoners had revolted and some S.S. were wounded in taming the storm. And then what to do with all the heap of corpses? A solution had been found in forcing the condemned to dig a ditch in order to then throw their corpses into it. But the prisoners' energy was too low and it took hours and hours to get a hole deep enough for the dogs not to come and pull the pieces of corpses out of the ground.

The invention of the Zyklon B gas was "providential," as someone recounted at the Nuremberg trials. It had allowed the elimination of thousands of people a day, in the silence of a closed and soundproofed room, with the modest expense of a little gas.

All this was unknown to my beloved parents who were enjoying the rivers and woods of Japan. They even ventured to have a third child. Indeed a daughter. Always hoping for a male who unfortunately did not arrive. Another little girl? What a disaster! My mother showed that she was worried, to indulge her husband. But she was so happy. Her maternal instinct knew no disappointments. Luckily he was informed enough to know that the sex of the unborn child does not depend on the mother but on the father. Who was to blame if not him, the brilliant professor, who escaped from Florence because of conflicts with his father, came to Japan with his young wife, hoping for a male descendant? Strange that he, who had known the difficulty of a bitter relationship with his father, in turn wanted to become the parent of a son. Perhaps in the memory of that little brother, Grato, who was always by his side as a child and whom he treated with the condescension and protection of a teenage father. Grato, the tall one. Grato, the redhead. He was different from his older brother: more timid, sweeter, milder, insecure. Because of this, he followed him step by step. But Grato had had the fortune to remain beside Grandmother Yoi. Even if he never spoke. From a lanky and judicious teenager he had become a taciturn and smiling young man. His silence was proverbial in the family. Seeing you after years of absence he was able to say only, "Oh, what's up?" and that was all. He married a beautiful Roman woman descended from Napoleon and had a daughter who also had a beautiful Napoleonic name, Letizia.

The third notebook ends in that '41 that presages many torments, with a postcard arrived from Italy. A photograph of Piazza Vittorio Emanuele in Florence. We assume it comes from grandmother Yoi, whom I'm glad I didn't see dead, like grandfather Antonio. I like to think of her standing, very thin as she was at the end, the long dress of oriental cloth, the gray hair gathered on the top of the head and then softly rolled down on the forehead, the eyes tender and delicate like butterflies, the mouth a little tightened by age. When we asked her how old she was, she answered: "I don't know, I stopped counting." She was an affable woman, great conversationalist, according to my mother.

Contrary to grandfather Antonio who preferred brooding silence. She, who was English, had an all-Mediterranean sociability, and he, Italian, seemed made of British stone, rigid and darkened by the Nordic winds. She blonde, he reddish, they'd made a handsome couple. He had fallen in love with the perfect face of an English woman, ten years his senior, but much younger in spirit and imagination, so much so as to face the ire of parents who detested the idea of a divorced woman with dependent children. A very elegant, sophisticated woman, but with something indomitable and wild at her heart's core. A woman "capable of anything," my grandfather said about her, with admiration but also a certain apprehension.

I like to imagine her with an arm raised, in an affectionate greeting to her grown granddaughters, to her now older son, who trudges like an old bear over the rugged mountains of the Tuscan coast. Their love, I always knew without anyone telling me, was as deep as the well of my country house.

There was no running water when I bought that piece of land between Flaminia and Cassia. So I called technicians to dig a well The workers began to drill down down for 20, 30, then 60 metres, but no water was found. "Ma'am, we can't find any vein here. You have to give it up. Let's build a cistern and then in the rain ..."

"No, let's keep digging," I replied, as much as I knew it would cost me dearly. And they resumed work. Dig, dig, after another week of trying they finally reached water, hurray! At a depth of one hundred and fifteen metres.

How wonderful to see that transparent liquid flow from the bowels of the earth: a fresh spring, with a strong flavour, which brings with it the scent of roots, of the hardest rocks, of the compressed earth, of the water kept pressured and bound for centuries. We had found a spring that would rise up, thanks to a powerful pump, to the interior of the house and would keep the flavour of minerals just awakened from sleep.

This is how I imagine Yoi's love for the little Fosco, who I see as a child, bedside his mother who kneels in front of him. This is how Grandfather Antonio carved them in a bas relief on the stone found in the Poggio Imperiale cemetery in Florence. For me it is definitely the most beautiful sculpture of grandfather's. Of his compositions I have never liked the shapes that were too demure and refined. The smoothness—somewhat lascivious—of his stone women, the indulgence of the pelvis, the predictable elegance of the mythical subjects, always in theatrical and rhetorical poses. Despite having a graceful and nimble hand, while knowing the trade well, the sculptor Antonio was a prisoner of virtuosity and his fundamental lack of freedom. That freedom of spirit from the bottom of his heart that reproached his wife, "the Englishwoman capable of anything." The woman he loved beyond himself, with fear and passion. She was a loyal and perfect wife, but had always retained something intangible and indomitable that he would never have been able to control as he would have liked.

The stele on the tomb of grandmother Yoi portrays her surmounted by a tangle of vines, next to her son. She is kneeling to be at the same height of the boy, perhaps two years old: her head covered by a handkerchief tied at the nape of her neck, a long skirt that wraps around her legs, her torso erect, slender. Her arms are outstretched towards the little boy who, one guesses, has been standing upright for a short time, but does so with boldness and stubbornness.

Next to the mother's knees are stone toys: a bear, a wagon with well-designed wheels, dice. Grandfather Antonio, who tended to smooth out the stony material making it polished and free of vigour, stopped here in time. For once he let his feelings transmit a stunned trembling to his hands. And he, too, was surprised and appreciative in the face of the mystery of this love. An absolute love that closed a circle from which he was excluded. But the miracle had been accomplished: the sculptor's chisel had traced the signs of that silent and great feeling, in simple humility, without wanting to judge, nor to prevaricate, to recompose, nor to explain, with the light detached respect of an artist in front of the enigma of an archaic, exclusive bond.

1950s. Every Sunday Yuki and I would go from the boarding school of the Santissima Annunziata al Poggio, hand in hand, towards the house of grandfather Antonio. He received us among his dahlias, and the statues of spring and autumn standing in sensual poses. Not a kiss, not a caress, not a smile, but a rebuke immediately: "How muddy your shoes are!" Or, "I see from your faces that you ran up the stairs, you look like two dirty, dishevelled peasants." It was not clear to what extent he was joking or serious. I am convinced that he had an affection for us, but his ethics forbade him to show any emotion, on pain of losing his self-respect. Every tenderness, every affection was for him a yielding to sentimentality and cheap romanticism. He was obsessed with an idea of formal perfection that could not be separated from education, disciplines and sacrifice.

Grandma Yoi continues to greet us with her arm raised. And I think I really regret not having found her on my return from Japan. I'm sure we would have understood each other. Mamà says she was very witty. And every now and then, when looking at grandfather, she'd say in a low voice, "A very fine man," as if to convince herself. I think she deemed him ruthless in his mania for perfection. But even so she treated him as he wanted to be treated, with respect and affection, keeping those distances that for her husband were part of every relationship "as it should be." Faithful to each other, they preserved the stable image of a close-knit and satisfied family. If she had extramarital temptations, she certainly sublimated them in intellectual encounters, as happened with Berenson who lived in the villa not far from the Tatti and loved to converse with the beautiful Yoi. If he betrayed her, it was, instead, with small ancillary lovers. Those bursts of sensuality that a good bourgeois secretly expresses, possibly with someone of lower social status, to whom he can appear, even in the most riotous intimacy, like a god, and who will have to thank him for the "honour."

1942. My mother's diary is now silent. She can't recall if she kept any trace of the daily news of 1942 and 1943, before entering the camp, where there certainly would have been no way to write or read.

"Perhaps I stopped keeping the diary about my daughters because the climate had changed. We lived in apprehension. The newspapers repeated words ordered by the government. And the people said, "Hitar, psuyoi-né," Hitler is powerful, right? with a mixture of admiration and fear.

"Those who were not in agreement with the German and Japanese invasions (in March Japan invaded the Dutch West Indies, the USA bombed Tokyo and in August the Salomon Islands occupied by the Japanese; in September began the Siege of Leningrad), those who were not in agreement remained silent, fearful of violent retribution. I was convinced that Hitler would not win. I don't know what gave me this conviction, but I was certain. Our situation was very delicate: we were part of an exchange program: so many Japanese scholarships and so many Italian ones. The diplomatic circles kept an eye on us. There were some at the embassy who thought like we did, the young Sforza attaché, for example. But even he couldn't speak."

My mother tries to remember the atmosphere of these traumatic years and her voice tightens. "The climate among Italians in Japan was changing: everyone looked at each other suspiciously. Some were skeptical towards fascism, like Sforza. Instead, Janelli, the ambassador, believed in it. He would stand there, rigid, and salute with his outstretched hand. Others, however, were beginning to doubt, like Cavalchini of San Severino, for example, the naval attaché who spoke without speaking, but made us understand that he hated Hitler and the senseless politics of the Italian Republic of Salò, subservient to the Germans and now without dignity and pride."

"But the news, the genuine ones, how did you get them?"

"Through the radio we listened to secretly. I also recall two French nationals who knew something about the killing of Jews in the extermination camps. One day, the woman whispered: you know that they burn people in ovens after having gassed them, women and children included? I said: That's not possible. Who told you this? It really seemed to be an invention. I thought it must be one of those numerous extreme rumours that circle during war. Who could possibly organize something as monstrous as the systematic extermination of an entire people, guilty only of belonging to a different religion? However this is exactly what occurred. I have no idea how our friends Baron Fain heard of it."

The news circled, evidently, but there was no official confirmation. Neither the Church nor the American government wanted to say how things stood until after the war, when photographers and filmmakers crossed to the other side of the barbed wire and discovered several survivors, who had escaped the genocide—all skin and bones—keeping warm under a blanket, their mouths in toothless smiles.

It's the final months of '41. My sister Toni is born after hours and hours of pain, the umbilical cord wrapped three times around her neck. That twisting within her refuge of flesh and blood seems, if I think of it today, a premonition of the terrible events that would soon change our lives.

"It seemed my last child would die and I with her. She was suffocating and didn't want to come out. They gave me an injection to induce labour, and I began once more … a pain so acute, I was unable to hold back my cries … I recall the Canadian nurse looking after me said, "Pleasure is paid with pain," an incredible punitive attitude towards women in labour. However, the hospital was well-kept, clean and efficient. After hours of suffering, Toni was born, purplish and half-asphyxiated by the cord cinched around her neck. When it came to the stitches, I asked for anaesthetic, and they replied it had all been sent to the front for the soldiers. Thus, I had to endure this, biting my lip.

"When Fosco arrived, I thought he might have objected to the third female child; instead he was pleased: better three girls than two girls and a boy, he said. And I was delighted. Paradoxically, Toni, who was born from such pain, was a happy, calm newborn. She never cried and as soon as she was able, she began to climb on everything."

I ask her if it's true, that they had in mind a different name for the last child. "Yes, we wanted to call her Kiku—chrysanthemum—but fascism did not permit foreign names, and in the end, we called her Antonella, which became Toni. We didn't want to have to repeat the vicissitudes of Yuki's christening: after giving the embassy the newborn's name, all the papers were sent to Italy, but were returned with the comment that Yuki was not a valid name for the birth certificate. Fosco refused to budge, saying he was free to name his daughter whatever he wanted. They would not accept this, and for months, Yuki remained without a name. In the end, we had to resort to Luisa, 'They'll have their way on paper, but we'll call her Yuki.' And in fact, Luisa has remained only the official name on her birth certificate. For us, she has always been Yuki.

"When it came to Toni, perhaps the question of her name didn't seem as important: the war was making itself felt with increasing arrogance, and Fosco didn't want to insist. We named her after her grandfather Antonio. However, I liked Kiku."

Who knows whether Toni's destiny might have been different had she been named Kiku—chrysanthemum. In Italy, the chrysanthemum is the flower of the dead; I didn't know if my little sister would have experienced symbolic hardships with that name. She certainly fit into the anthropological strategy of my father: if she is born in Japan, she will be partly Japanese and her name will establish a geographic reality, which though not aligned with her birth certificate, will be revelatory of a cultural belonging.

In Japan, the chrysanthemum is a sacred flower, a flower symbolizing the sun's longevity and heat. Its petals, they say, are arranged in the shape of solar rays and thus imitate the star of life. "Oh! At Nara / The scent of chrysanthemums / And old Buddhas!" writes the poet Basho in 1673. "Furthermore, explains Chevalier and Gheerbrant, "The chrysanthemum, *kiku*, evokes through a homonym, the word *kiku-ri*, which means listening to the truth, from which is derived *Kukuri*, the name of one of the primordial *kami*."

For the Chinese, instead, the chrysanthemum is the autumn flower and represents the time of rest after harvest. Among flowers, the philosopher Chu T'un-yi says, the chrysanthemum is "the one that conceals itself and escapes the world." Nothing could be more true as it pertains to my sister Toni, who hides under leaves like a solitary snail that has lost its shell and doesn't want to get wet.

She writes with grace and vigour, but hides the pages, like Jane Austen did in her time, almost as if writing were a sin of vanity. She has passionately divided herself between writing and motherhood. She has two grown daughters, Mujah and Nour, of which one is a theatre actor in New York, and the other studies anthropology at the university in Rome.

Toni has instinctively followed the paternal project of anthropological adherence to places of suffering and joy chosen by study or passion. She set up house in Morocco, marrying an elegant Arab painter; has lived many years in Casablanca, writing and organizing festivals of the arts. Her daughters are as fluent in Arabic and French as they are in Italian. At the beginning of 2001, her elder

daughter gave birth to a boy, Gabriele Fosco, son of the charm-
ing and accomplished New York actor of Irish origin, Daniel
McDonald.

"November of '42. The Japanese newspapers spoke of the naval battle of Guadalcanal (an island in the Solomon archipelago) where so
many young soldiers had died. I could not feed Toni, because my
breasts had no milk. I think it may have been because of that terrible labour in childbirth," my mother says, appropriately continuing
the diary she didn't write back then, digging into her crystalline,
tempestuous memory.

The word 'Guadalcanal' transports me to distant lost days.
Guadalcanal, but what does it remind me of? I read it was a naval
battle between the Japanese and Americans in the stretch of sea
between the islands of Florida and Tulagi; a battle that lasted from
the 11th to the 15th of November, during the week of my birthday.
The small war planes had to destroy the airport the Americans had
seized from the Japanese in August.

If I close my eyes, I can see them: they fly low, and are slow
and clumsy and dark like large pregnant ducks. That's how I would
have come to know them in the sky of the Nagoya concentration
camp. In those bellies are the eggs, and now they'll come out and
spit red yolks on the heads of the crowd, I told myself. I really saw
those eggs—pale against a pale sky—emerge from the belly, one
by one, and slide towards earth. However the shells did not open
to spill soft yellow tasty yolks, but to spit out small iron monsters
and fire that caused wounds and death to whomever found himself
within range. How many times I heard the hissing of splinters over
my head while we ran to hide in the trench doubling as an air-raid
shelter. The deafening sound of motors in tandem at night is still
there, inside my ear. It was the sound of fear.

But the night of November 13 of '42 in Guadalcanal something
went wrong for the ducks whose bellies were full of metal eggs. A
dim light lit up the edges of the sky. A torpedo approached like an
arrow and dead-centre hit the airplane, which spun then fell in a

column of smoke. The cocky ducks of death were caught mid-act and struck. It would have been the first in a series of setbacks that brought the definitive defeat of Japan.

"I didn't have a drop of milk for baby Toni Kiku," my mother explains. "I didn't know what to do. Dr. Wittemberg told me to give her cow's milk, but where was I to find cow's milk? And so, I began to search the entire city and its environs and in the end, I found a farmer who had a pregnant cow. I told him about the baby without milk, and he was kind enough to let me milk the cow. In general, Japanese civilians were generous and hospitable. Only the military was cruel, sadistic and stupidly nationalistic. Our nanny, Moriokasan, for example, was the only one among our friends who had the courage to come and visit us in the concentration camp, risking arrest. And in fact, she was beaten. And the second time, they wouldn't even let her approach."

"Moriokasan had a soldier husband who was in Hiroshima when the atomic bomb exploded. Miraculously, he survived. I remember his stories retold: he was in the barracks, eating rice and *zukemono* when he saw an immense light, then everything began to shake around him, followed by an absolute darkness into which he passed out. When he regained consciousness some minutes later, he found himself inside a small artificial lake, about a kilometre from the barracks. The immersion in water had saved him from the firestorm. Of the thousands of his fellow soldiers all that remained were shadows seared on stones. He survived a few more years, until the residual radiation of the blast took effect, and he died of a form of cancer common to the survivors of the bombing of Hiroshima.

"They called it 'black rain,' that which fell after the bomb, and against which the citizens who rushed to help the wounded spread throughout the city didn't think to defend themselves. That black water was radioactive and continued to kill for years and years. Like a long, unjust death, it gathered people in the midst of the euphoria of reconstruction, unrelentingly attacking their limbs until they became gnawed as if by a greedy, obscene mouth. All because the

Americans withheld warnings about the dangers of the bomb's aftermath. No one in Japan knew the consequences of radiation contained in the drops of rain that washed the sky after the atomic mushroom."

"I would add two-thirds water to the milk, because it was too fatty, and I could give it to her without boiling it, so as not to lose the vitamins, as I had been told by Wittemberg. And Toni, drinking the milk of the Japanese cow, became very strong. She grew in front of our eyes, laughed and played; she was an extraordinary girl. Only a year later, in the Nagoya concentration camp, did she turn into an angry, defiant child, constantly yelling: I'm hungry! I'm hungry! so much so, that everyone begged me to silence her, but how? I worried, because she had no new teeth. During our entire stay in the camp, she didn't grow even an inch. My menstrual periods stopped. And we were all full of parasites. Do you remember how we deloused each other like monkeys …? The only difference is that we didn't eat those disgusting bugs once squished … even if almost, because of our great hunger, we could have …," my delightful mother says, laughing, making black humour out of that atrocity.

The filth, the parasites are things that humiliate the body and render it greedy and wild. I still recall the poisoning from worms that swelled the belly and emerged from our bums instead of feces, because there was nothing to expel. Damned worms took advantage of our weakness to lodge in our intestines, and eat every kernel of rice they found. And I recall the shame of seeing those lice dance on the bed in the morning, fat with our blood. I had become excellent at catching them. But as many as I squished came out of the folds in our clothes, from the seams of our underwear. No matter how much my mother washed everything over and over, we remained infested.

Yuki can now stand with help for quite a few seconds and does not want to talk. She holds out her hand when she wants to be picked up, and kicks furiously. She can sit unaided, but she falls to one side, and needs cushions arranged around her.

And a few days later, a huge title on the diary page:

YUKI'S FIRST WORDS
  July 5th. Almost a year. For the first time, Yuki is standing on her own.
  Words: Tatta! Odì. Dacia-ciàn.
  July 14 onnicià (connichiwa)
  àdà *(ya-da)*
  babài *(banzai) celebration, best wishes for a thousand years of good*
health and immortality
  o-bàba *(obasan) the nanny*

One day, in the convent where we lived after we were transferred to Tempaku from Nagoya, a monk died. I still see him, seated, leaning against the wall, his chin against his chest. The worn clothes, the hollow face, the small feet wrapped in the soiled 'tabi,' he had died and no one had noticed. Not even we children, who thought he had fallen asleep. Until the monk's grandchild, the small and kind Keiko, cried, "Look!" From the body of the man, from his threadbare clothes descended thousands of bugs, that quickly formed into disciplined columns and headed for the door. Proof that the blood was cooling. Proof that there was nothing more to eat.

"Remember to explain that I didn't go to a concentration camp simply to follow a beloved husband," my mother says, petting her white cat to whom she speaks as if he were a baby. "The Japanese military authority called both of us, Papà and me, separately, and asked us to sign up for the Republica di Salò. Fosco answered, 'I am an official of the Alpini and can't sign anything against them.' On my own, I said Nazism didn't concur with my ideas, that I did not like racism. We stared at each other from afar, Fosco and I, and understood we'd made the same choice. From then on, they locked us in a house under police watch. We could not go out, nor telephone, nor write to anyone. You came to me with a branch of citronella, do you remember? 'Smell, Mamà, it will cheer you up,' you said.

"At the start, they wanted to separate us. But then the wife of the mayor of Nagoya, who was Christian, came to our rescue. Who knows what would have happened if they had put you in a school for children of 'traitors': this is how they called us with outright contempt. The wife of the mayor of Nagoya said, 'No, leave them together, you can't separate a mother from her children.' And so, after those initial days of house arrest, they came to get us, and take us towards the south."

But this is another story and falls outside the love diaries written by my mother and resurrected by chance from my father's Florentine dresser. I promised my sister that I'd let her tell that story. Therefore, I ask my readers to be patient to listen to what follows the events thus far: the years in the concentration camp, so intense and painful, the war, the daily life of the camp. For many years, I tried to tell this story, but I have always paused, breathless, at the edge of the woods, in both shame and dismay. Suddenly in front of me appears a faceless man, who walks quickly. And I run, run, until I reach a truck and I tell the driver about the terrible encounter. And he turns his empty face towards me, and says, "Like me?"

About the Author

DACIA MARAINI is one of Italy's leading contemporary writers. Novelist, poet, dramatist and journalist, she was born in Fiesole in the province of Florence in 1936, and burst onto the Italian literary and cultural scene in the 1960s, where she combined a brilliant style with a sharp critique of contemporary society. A prolific writer, she has produced 21 novels and as many plays, plus short stories, poetry, screenplays, and narrative journalism. London's *Guardian* newspaper called her "a novelist of grand ambition and intense feeling and, always, an enthralling storyteller."

Among her best known works, besides *Donna in Guerra (Woman at War)*, which is widely considered a manifesto of Italian feminism, are *Mio marito (My Husband)*, *Memorie di una ladra* (1972), *Il treno per Helsinki (The Train for Helsinki)* (1984), *Isolina* (1985), and *La lunga vita di Marianna Ucria (The Silent Duchess)* (1990), *Dolce* (1997) and *Buio* (1999), a collection of short stories. She has won awards for her work, including the Formentor Prize for *L'età del malessere* (1963); the *Premio Fregene* for *Isolina* (1985); the *Premio Campiello* and Book of the Year Award for *La lunga vita di Marianna Ucrìa* (1990); and the Premio Strega for *Buio* (1999). Her plays include *Il ricatto a teatro* (1970), *Maria Stuarda* (1975), *I sogni di Clitennestra* (1981), *Veronica, meretrice e scrittora* (1991). Her poetry includes *Se amando troppo* (1998) and *Viaggiando col passo di volpe (Traveling in the Gait of a Fox)* (2003). Her most recent book is a novella, *Trio* (2020) set in Messina, Sicily in 1743, during the plague that killed 40,000 to 50,000 people.

Fifteen of Maraini's books and stories have been adapted for films, and she has been the subject of as many documentaries.

Maraini is among the foremost women writers in Italy to have taken on the traditional social role of the male intellectual—equally at home in the university lecture circuit, on popular television, in the theatre and poetry scene. She remains an unapologetic progressive and feminist; and—in the best tradition of the European public intellectual—has continued her political activism for over four decades.

In 2020, Maraini won the International Literary Award Viareggio Rèpaci—Premio Alla Carriera, "a Lifetime Achievement Award to DACIA MARAINI, a masterful writer with a long and fruitful narrative, lyrical, essay and dramaturgical path, particularly attentive, from a historical and documentary perspective, to major social issues, the condition of women, and childhood problems."

Her life's work was shortlisted for the 2011 Man Booker International Prize and she has been nominated for the Nobel Prize for Literature.

About the Translator

GENNI GUNN is an author, musician and translator. Born in Trieste, she came to Canada when she was eleven. She has published fourteen books: four novels—*The Cipher, Solitaria* (nominated for the Giller Prize), *Tracing Iris* (made into a film, *The Riverbank),* and *Thrice Upon a Time* (finalist for the Commonwealth Writers' Prize); three short story collections—the recent *Permanent Tourists, Hungers, On The Road;* three poetry collections—*Accidents* (finalist for the DiCicco Poetry Award and the SCWES book award), *Faceless* and *Mating in Captivity* finalist for the Gerald Lampert Award), and a collection of personal essays, *Tracks: Journeys in Time and Place.* As well, she has written an opera libretto, *Alternate Visions* (music by John Oliver), produced by Chants Libres in Montreal in 2007, and translated from Italian three collections of poems, two by renowned Italian author, Dacia Maraini—*Devour Me Too* (finalist for the John Glassco Translation Prize) and *Travelling in the Gait of a Fox* (finalist for the Premio Internazionale Diego Valeri for Literary Translation), and *Text Me* by Corrado Calabró. She lives in Vancouver.

(Endnotes)

1 Dacia Maraini, "Tokyo di notte: una donna al computer," (Tokyo at Night: A Woman on the Computer"), part of the series "Ritorno in Giappone/1 - Dacia Maraini e il padre Fosco sui luoghi dove vissero in prigionia dal '43 al '46." ("Return to Japan/1- Dacia Maraini and Her Father Fosco in the Places Where They Lived in Captivity from 1943 to 1946"). Corriere della Sera, December 11, 1990. Translation by Michelangelo La Luna. "La prima persona che incontriamo andando a Nagoya è Sawako Morioka, la balia che ci ha tenute in braccio me e le mie sorelle negli anni della guerra. È piccola, ha ottant'anni ma le sue guance sono ancora rosee e la sua risata allegra. Ci abbracciamo. Ci scambiamo dei regali. Purtroppo io non parlo più il giapponese e il suo italiano è incomprensibile. "Stanco biaggio?" mi ripete massaggiandomi il collo indolenzito. Le sue dita corrono veloci e sapienti. Ripenso a com'era da giovane, robusta, piccola, festosa, capace di andare in giro portando mia sorella Toni legata sulla schiena, mia sorella Yuki in braccio e me tirata per la mano. È stata la sola che abbia avuto il coraggio di sfidare la polizia per venire a trovarci nel campo di concentramento. E per questo è stata picchiata e diffidata."

2 Fosco Maraini, "Mèta: un Vieusseux-Asia", in *Firenze, il Giappone e l'Asia orientale: Atti del Convegno Internazionale di Studi, Firenze, 25-27 marzo 1999*, edited by Adriana Boscaro e Maurizio Bossi, «Gabinetto Scientifico Letterario G. P. Vieusseux, Centro Romantico – Studi 10», Firenze, Leo S. Olschki, 2001, p. XIV. Later published in Fosco Maraini e Franco Marcoaldi, *Pellegrino in Asia: opere scelte*, Milano, Mondadori 2007, p. CXII.«Voi giapponesi cosa fareste in un caso del genere? - chiedemmo all'uffiziale - Stareste

con l'imperatore o col primo ministro?» «Ovviamente con l'imperatore!» fu l'immediata risposta. «Ebbene anche noi vi imitiamo, stiamo col re» «Nel qual caso ci dispiace molto - fece il commissario alzandosi - *mais vous devenez ennemis...* e dovrete soffrirne le conseguenze. Preparatevi per l'internamento».

3 *Ibidem.* "Io avevo raccolto già un migliaio di volumi, oltre a molto materiale etnografico. Chiusi il tutto in una cinquantina di cassette da brace (come usavano allora in Giappone) sperando che qualche miracolo le salvasse. E il miracolo avvenne! Nel frangente ci venne in aiuto il vicedirettore dell'Istituto Francese di Cultura di Kyoto, l'amico Jean-Pierre Hauchecorne (purtroppo recentemente deceduto) il quale si portò via le cassette e le nascose nelle ampie cantine dell'istituto stesso."

4 Dacia Maraini. *La nave per Kobe*, 165. All quotations in English of *La nave per Kobe* are taken from Genni Gunn's translation of the book. An excerpt of this translation was previously published in *Beloved Writing. Fifty Years of Engagement. Writing Like Breathing. An Homage to Dacia Maraini*, vol. I, edited and compiled by Michelangelo La Luna. Part of the series SOPHIA, III, Literature 2, directed by Michelangelo La Luna. Barcelona-Trento: List-Lab International Editorial Strategies Laboratory, 2016, pp. 15-21. "1942. Il diario di mia madre è ormai muto. Lei non ricorda se ha tenuto qualche traccia delle cronache quotidiane per l'anno 1942 e per l'anno 1943, prima di entrare nel campo, dove certamente non c'era stato più modo di scrivere né di leggere.

Forse ha smesso di compilare il diario sulle figlie perché il clima era cambiato. Si viveva nella preoccupazione. La stampa ripeteva le parole d'ordine del governo. E la gente diceva "Hitar, tsuyoi-né," Hitler è forte vero? con un misto di ammirazione e di paura.

5 Maraini Dacia, "Why Do I Write?", in *Dacia Maraini and Her Literary Journey*, edited and compiled by Michelangelo La Luna, co-edited by Angela Pitassi, *Writing Like Breathing*, vol. IV, p. 28.

6   Dacia Maraini interviewed by Alessandra Troncana, "Il Giappone di Fosco Maraini: 'Quando papà si tagliò il dito per salvarci dagli aguzzini'," *Corriere della Sera*, July 27, 2016.

7   Fosco Maraini, "Mèta: un Vieusseux-Asia", XIV; *Pellegrino in Asia: opere scelte*, CXII. "Un anno dopo ecco un altro miracolo: gli americani dell'armata d'occupazione ci offrirono gratis il ritorno in Italia - con tutte le famose cassette. Fu una traversata lunghissima di due oceani; prima il Pacifico, poi il canale di Panama, infine l'Atlantico con l'ultimo sbarco nel porto francese di Le Havre. Restava ancora il viaggio da Le Havre a Firenze... Qui altro colpo fortunato: l'ambasciatore italiano, col quale viaggiavamo, aggiunse i nostri bagagli e le famose 50 cassette, al cargo della missione. Insomma, col maggio del 1946, di miracolo in miracolo eravamo a Firenze senza aver perso nulla - e con la sola spesa di qualche mancia agli svariati facchini lungo il percorso. La collezione etnografica venne da me poco dopo donata al Museo d'Antropologia al Palazzo Nonfinito; ed il nocciolo della biblioteca era al sicuro nella casa di famiglia, fuori porta Romana, a Firenze."

8   Dacia Maraini, "Why do I write", 17.

9   The diaries were later also published as Topazia Alliata. *Ricordi d'arte e prigionia di Topazia Alliata*, edited by Toni Maraini (Palermo: Sellerio, 2003); on the same topic, also see Toni Maraini. *La lettera da Benares*, Palermo: Sellerio Editore, 2007.

10   Maraini, *La nave per Kobe*, 7. "Il passato ha la capacità di saltarti addosso a tradimento attraverso una fotografia, una lettera/ Ti racconta di un tempo che non c'è più e che pure si fa vivo ai tuoi occhi con una vivacità assolutamente insospettate. Favoleggia nel tuo orecchio di una parte di te ormai sparita. Che credevi del tutto morta e che invece stava in letargo in qualche angolo della memoria. Sono ia questa bambina, mi cido, ma non sono più io."

11   Francesco Petrarca, *Le rime*. *"Passa la nave mia colma d'oblio /
per aspro mare, a mezza notte il verno /[...] La vela rompe un vento
umido eterno / di sospir, di speranze e di desio."*

12   Vincenzo Caldarelli, Passato da Poesie. *"I ricordi, queste ombre
troppo lunghe / del nostro breve corpo."*

13   Maraini. *La nave per Kobe*, p. 177. "Quindi chiedo ai miei let-
tori di pazientare per ascoltare il seguito delle vicende fin qui seguite.
Gli anni del campo di concentramento, così intensi e dolorosi, la
guerra, la vita quotidiana del campo. Per tanti anni ho cercato di
raccontarla questa storia ma sul limitare del bosco mi sono sempre
fermata, col fiato mozzo, un senso di pudore e di sbigottimento
insieme. Davanti a me improvvisamente appare un uomo senza
faccia che cammina rapido. E io corro, corro, finché raggiungo un
carretto e racconto al carrettiere il terribile incontro. E lui volge
verso di me la sua faccia vuota e dice "Come me?""

14   Maraini, *La nave per Kobe*, 11. "Più tardi, in una sala come
quella, avrei conosciuto, per via cinematografica, una Ingrid
Bergman dalle luci soffuse riflesse negli occhi morbidi, dai riccioli
castani che guizzano attorno al collo. Qual è l'incantesimo che ti
allaccia ad una attrice dal sorriso flou e la voce cristallina? In lei
vedevo mia madre giovane: le gambe snelle, il taglio del tailleur
stretto in vita, le scarpe dal tacco ortopedico. La vedevo camminar
veloce, con un cappello di feltro color castagna che le nascondeva
in parte la fronte e mi pareva di scorgere una intera generazione di
donne dal piede segreto e l'occhio scintillante."

15   Elkann Alain and Moravia Alberto, *Vita di Moravia*, Milano:
Bompiani, 1990, p. 212. "Elsa dava il meglio di sé in circostanze
eccezionali, di emergenza. Ma nei viaggi aveva la particolarità di
portarsi dietro il rapporto psicologico che è proprio della vita quotidiana. Potevamo anche andare in capo al mondo, ma sembrava

che fossimo tutt'ora a via dell'Oca. Non viaggiava, "Elsa, si spostava, ecco tutto. Con Dacia, invece, ho veramente viaggiato, in un senso in qualche modo avventuroso che non è tanto fatto di avventure ma di completa dimenticanza del mondo stabile e ben definito lasciato in patria... Ho viaggiato come si sogna... ho finalmente viaggiato con abbandono e scoperta. Non è senza significato che per festeggiare la nostra unione scegliemmo di fare il giro del mondo. Forse fu una specie di scommessa; in realtà fu anche soprattutto una fame alfine soddisfatta di spazio e di libertà."

16   Maraini Dacia. *La nave per Kobe*, 16. "Ma proprio in quel momento arriva l'amministratore del vescovo, tutto vestito di scuro – nero su nero, elegantissimo – e ci mette in mano il conto. Restiamo a bocca aperta. Il vescovo aveva conteggiato perfino l'acqua per lavarsi e il tutto ammontava al prezzo di un albergo a quattro stelle. Altro che òbolo! Abbiamo pagato e siamo partiti, senza neanche vederlo, il vescovo che, alle dieci di mattina, ancora dormiva."

17   For more information, see Tonino Tornitore, "Moravia e l'India", in Alberto Moravia, *Un'Idea dell'India*, Milano: Bompiani, 1962.

18   The trip in India and the madras t-shirts are also mentioned in Dacia Maraini, *La Grande Festa*. Milano: Rizzoli BUR, 2011, p. 12.

19   Maraini. *La nave per Kobe*, 20

20   Maraini. *La nave per Kobe*, 125

21   In Italian, a metalanguage of assonances and inventions; a linguistic game full of deep echoes.

22   Maraini. *La nave per Kobe*, 25-26

23   Maraini. *La nave per Kobe*, 109-110

Printed by Imprimerie Gauvin
Gatineau, Québec